Dry Fly Fishing

Dave Hughes

photographed by Jim Schollmeyer

flies tied by John Rodriguez

Frank Amato

PORTLAND

Dedication

To my Sister:
Frances Grace Burham

Acknowledgements

Guido Rahr, Jr. gracefully performed many of the casts for the photos in this book. His gracious family provided access to some of the water where the photos were shot. John Rodriguez, given short notice, tied the beautiful flies for the plates. Ted Leeson braved the brawling Madison River to make cast after cast while Jim Schollmeyer took shot after shot. I always owe more thanks to Jim than I can ever explain.

Dave Hughes co-authored the classic *Western Hatches* with Rick Hafele. His other books include *Deschutes, The Yellowstone River and Its Angling, Strategies for Stillwater,* and the four-book *Strategies for Streams* series. In 1983 Dave was founding president of Oregon Trout. In 1985 he was awarded the Lew Jewett Memorial Life Membership in the Federation of Fly Fishers. In 1992 the Flyfisher's Club of Oregon presented the Vernon S. "Pete" Hidy award to Dave for his significant contributions to angling literature. He makes his home in Portland, Oregon.

Jim Schollmeyer is author of *Deschutes Hatches.* His photos have appeared in *Field & Stream, Fly Fisherman* Magazine, *Fly Rod & Reel, Flyfishing, Salmon Trout Steelheader,* and many others. His previous book pictorial projects include *Deschutes,* and the acclaimed photos in Randle Scott Stetzer's *Flies: The Best One Thousand.* Schollmeyer is a well-known guide on Oregon's Deschutes River. He makes his home in Salem, Oregon.

Published in 1994 by Frank Amato Publications Inc.,
P.O. Box 82112, Portland, Oregon 97282
(503) 653-8108

Softbound ISBN: 1-878175-68-8

Book Design: Tony Amato

Printed in Hong Kong

10 9 8 7 6 5 4 3

Table of Contents

Chapter 1

❧

Song of the Dry Fly

*D*ry fly fishing is the easiest of all the fly fishing methods to learn. It's also among the most effective. This combination of ease added to effectiveness creates one of the finest reasons to take up dry fly fishing. It's far from the only reason.

The dry fly method is easiest to learn because the equipment needed is simple and everything happens right up top, where you can easily see it. You need only a rod, reel, line, leader and fly. The strike is visible, and you can set the hook instantly, which incites the riot that is a fight with a fish. The dry fly method is so effective against trout because dry flies are tied to resemble the aqautic and terrestrial insects that trout make a living eating throughout most of the fishing season. This is also the time of the year when beauty is best in the places where trout are found.

You'd be foolish to remove beauty from your list of reasons to take up dry fly fishing. The flies themselves, like the insects they resemble, have a beauty that is sometimes striking, more often subtle. It resides in pert form and precise balance, in color and cockiness. If you learn to tie dries, you can create this beauty yourself.

Another beauty about dry flies is the way they allow you to admire the beauty of trout. You'll inherit the distant beauty that they display during the fight: their strength and leaping and dashing. You'll also observe the close kind of beauty awarded only to those who hold trout in their hands: their slenderness and sleek form that follow the function of living in swift waters.

Trout waters are the main propellant to a dry fly fisher's life. Trout dash to dries in the plunge pools of tiny mountain creeks. They rise with bold splashes to dries drifted on the riffles and pools of favorite trout streams. They calmly intercept dry flies in the shallows of the biggest rivers. Trout sip daily hatches of dainty insects and nip at their imitations on beautiful spring creeks and meadow streams. They cruise in pods and sprinkle rise rings across the surfaces of lakes and ponds.

All of these separate beauties—of the flies, of the trout, and of the places where you cast dry flies to entice the trout—get condensed into the single instant of the strike to the dry fly. Spray is tossed into the air. You see a flash of color inside the strike. You feel the sudden pulsing of life in your hand as you raise the rod to set the hook. The strike, and the shout it incites, are merely the cymbols clashing in the song of the dry fly. Most of the song is sung in the soft notes of water flowing above clean stones.

No matter what part of the world you live in, the song of the dry fly is always played in places where fishing is unburdened and simple, and when beauty is at its best.

Mayfly dun . . .

Imitation versus Presentation

Fly fishing writers enjoy grand arguments over the importance of exact imitation in their flies as opposed to perfect presentation in their casting. Some declare imitation to be everything, presentation to be nothing at all. Others declare presentation everything, and call casting exact imitations an excellent way to waste time.

The argument for presentation is persuasive. If your cast spooks fish, you're never going to catch them. If you place your dry delicately onto the water, and it arrives in front of the fish floating as freely as an unfettered natural, most trout will take any fly that reminds them about what they've been eating. The beneficial result: you spend your time learning to cast rather than learning to identify insects. You can carry just a few flies rather than bulging boxes of them.

The argument for imitation can be just as compelling. When feeding, trout key on certain characteristics of the insect species they're eating. If your fly lacks those key characteristics, trout will examine it but turn away from it no matter how well it's presented. If you've got the right fly, and cast it persistently enough, everything is bound to become perfect on one of your casts, and you'll catch the trout.

The mistake both sides make is to separate imitation and presentation. They are two halves of the same thing: making your dry fly look like something alive and good to eat to a trout. You must first select a fly that looks like food to the fish. Then you must present it so that it looks like something living, on the water. Get just one of the two right and you might catch a few fish. Accomplish both together and you'll begin to catch lots of trout, and larger trout.

At first you should lean toward presentation. Learn to cast well, and to present your flies delicately. Trout will often take the wrong fly fished right. They will rarely take the right fly fished wrong. This early concentration on presentation also allows you to simplify your fly pattern selection as you ease into the sport.

The more often trout are fished over, the more selective they become. As you move to more popular and heavily fished waters, you must become more precise in both halves of the equation: imitation and presentation.

. . . and its imitation.

You must also pay more attention to both factors as you move from rough water to smoother water. You can wade right up next to trout in pocket water and riffles. An awkward presentation is not likely to disturb them; an exact imitation is not likely to float well enough to fool them. Move to a slick-topped flat, or to a lake or pond, and trout are more wary and more selective. To catch them, you must select a fly that imitates what they have been eating, and you must present it with accuracy and delicacy.

As a hatch gets heavy, and trout concentrate more and more on a single species of insect, they tend to ignore everything else. Fishing over hatches forces you into an emphasis on imitation, but doesn't allow you to ignore presentation. That's why the argument between imitation and presentation persists. Some people fish most often where hatches are rarely heavy. Presentation is most important to them. Other people seek out situations where trout rise to hatches almost daily. Imitation becomes most important to them.

If you want to be able to take trout wherever you find them, then you'll be best served by learning to solve both halves of the equation: imitation and presentation.

A careful presentation is at least as important as the correct imitation.

Chapter 2

❧

Tackle for Dry Fly Fishing

*I*n fly casting, the rod lofts the line and carries it in the air. The line turns the leader over at the end of the cast. The leader sets the fly lightly onto the water. All parts of the dry fly outfit must be in balance: the rod must have the right stiffness to lift and carry the line; the line must be the right weight to load the rod; the leader must be the right taper to turn over the fly at the end of the cast.

The rod, line, and leader must also be in balance with the size dry fly that you intend to cast. Large and bushy dry flies

Large fly requires a stout outfit.

have lots of air resistance. It takes a stiff leader to turn them over, and a relatively heavy line to push them through the air. The heavy line requires a strong rod to loft it.

Small and light dry flies have little air resistance. They turn over easily at the end of long, fine leaders. A light line will carry them in the air. The rod required to cast the light line is light and feathery when held in the hand.

Your dry fly outfit should be chosen based on the size flies you'll be casting, not based on the size stream you intend to fish. Many small streams have the roughest water. You'll want to fish them with big and bushy dries that float well and are easy to see. Hence you'll want a fairly heavy outfit. Many large rivers have smooth water and hatches of tiny insects. You'll want to fish them with small flies and the lightest, most delicate outfit.

Light (#4), medium (#5), and heavy (#6) rods.

Small fly is best fished with a light outfit.

Dry Fly Rods

Choose a rod that performs best for the kind of dry fly fishing you do most. If your fishing will be on a wide variety of water types, in all winds and weathers, and more often with large flies than with small ones, you'll want a fairly heavy searching rod. If you'll be fishing primarily over insect hatches, with small flies, a light presentation rod will serve you better.

Searching Rod: A rod balanced to a double taper or weight-forward 6-weight line will handle the bushiest dry flies. It will be perfect for the middle range of hackled and hairwing dries, in sizes 10 through 14. With care you can present small dry flies with it, down to size 18 or so. It should be a quality graphite rod, 8-1/2 to 9 feet long. The action should be moderately fast to fast, for a brisk casting stroke.

Presentation Rod: To handle size 14 to 20 dries, choose a graphite rod balanced to a double taper 4-weight line. A 3-weight will work fine if you rarely fish in wind. The presentation rod should be 8 to 9 feet long for control of the line in the air and on the water. The action should be moderate. A stiff, fast rod will rob you of accuracy and delicacy.

Compromise Rod: A rod that snugs between the searching and presentation rods will allow you to boss the largest flies, yet still be delicate with the tiniest. It will let you fish dries without problems in the widest range of conditions. If you're going to buy just one rod, this is the one with which most trout guides and writers do most of their own dry fly fishing. It's an 8-1/2 to 9 foot graphite balanced to a 5-weight double-taper line, with a moderately fast action.

Rod length is important for control after the cast.

Rod Action: The best dry fly rods have moderate to slightly fast actions. Average graphite rods on the market today are too fast (too stiff) for dry fly fishing. They're designed for distance, not delicacy. To find out if a rod has the right dry fly action, give it this test before you buy it: string the rod with the right line, then spend a few minutes casting at specific aiming points just 15 to 25 feet away. Cast 45 to 60 feet only after you've determined that the rod will handle short casts softly and accurately. If it won't, don't buy it no matter how far you can haul off and cast with it.

Control is nearly always more important than distance.

Dry Fly Lines

Always use a floating line for dry fly fishing. Buy the best you can afford. You must choose between a double taper line and a weight forward line.

Double Taper Line: The 70 foot mid-section of a 90 foot double taper line is a constant diameter. Ten feet at each end tapers to a fine point, allowing energy to transfer delicately to the leader. The double taper is best for control of the cast in the air and on the water. It is accurate and delicate. You can mend line to control the drift of the fly. Its only drawback is distance casting: 60 feet and more. Since distance is rarely important when fishing dries, the double taper line is the best choice for most of your dry fly fishing.

Weight Forward Line: The weight forward taper has most of its casting weight in the first 30 feet. It has a short front taper, and 60 to 70 feet of thin running line. The weight forward line is better for distance casting because you can shoot lots of line into the cast. You sacrifice some control in the air, and lots of control on the water: it's difficult to mend line with the weight forward line. For the largest rivers, especially when you fish big dry flies to the banks from a boat, arm your searching rod with a weight forward 6- or even 7-weight line.

Rod/Line Rating: Fly rods are rated to balance a specific double taper line. If you use a weight forward line on the same rod, it will usually require one that is a single weight heavier, for example a WF6F line on a rod rated as a 5-weight. Even when you choose a double taper, be sure to cast the rod with the rated line and one that is a single weight heavier. Often the heavier line balances the rod better for the short casts most common in dry fly fishing.

Line Color: If trout see your line in the air, they'll spook no matter what color the line. Hence a bright color is just as effective as a dark one. It's usually best to choose a line color that is easy to see on the water, since it helps you follow the drift of your fly. The modern bright oranges and yellows are fine. More traditional ivory and peach have been found to be excellent over the years.

Double Taper 3, 4, & 5, and Weight Forward 5, 6, & 7 lines.

Cleaning The Line: If your floating line gets dirty, it starts to sink and fails to shoot cleanly through the guides. Use any of the many available line dressings to clean it at the start of the day, and any time it gets dirty during the day. If your casting starts to get slightly difficult, clean your line.

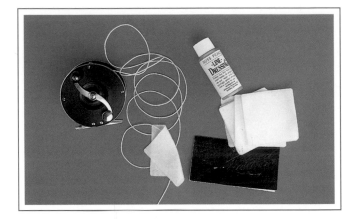

Dry Fly Reels

Select your reel only after you've chosen your rod and line, since those are the critical parts that must be in balance. Once you've picked out the rod and line, then choose a reel that balances the rod in both weight and appearance. You don't want a reel that is too heavy, or one that looks bulky and outsized when attached to the reel seat. You can achieve both kinds of balance—in weight and aesthetics—by choosing the lightest and smallest reel that will hold your fly line plus 100 yards of 20 pound test Dacron backing line.

The reel should be a single action: one turn of the handle causes one revolution of the spool. Multiplying reels are an unnecessary expense. Automatic reels are an unnecessary weight. Unless you plan to play lots of large trout, a single action reel with a simple click and paul drag system is all you'll ever need. If your plans include exotic trips after lots of large trout, you might want to buy a reel with a disc drag.

For dry fly fishing, keep your reel simple, functional, durable, and light. Simplicity can cost money: buy the best single action reel you can afford.

Single action reels.

Dry Fly Leaders

The main function of the leader is to render invisible the connection between your line and the fly. It's just as important that the leader be properly constructed to transfer energy of the cast from the line to the fly. The leader must also allow your dry fly to float freely and naturally. If you use a leader with a tippet that is too heavy for the size fly you're casting, the leader will cause drag. If you use a tippet that is too light, the cast will not straighten. That is why your leader must be in near perfect balance with your outfit, and with your fly. (Refer to tippet chart on this page.)

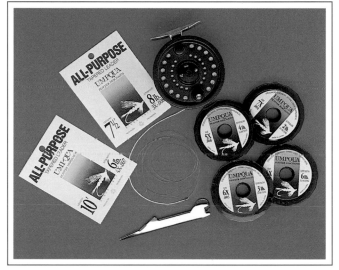

Fix a leader butt to line, and carry tippet spools.

Three Parts of the Leader: A leader is built with a butt, a tapered mid-section, and a tippet. The function of the long butt is to accept the energy of the line. The function of the short mid-section is to transfer that energy to the tippet. The function of the tippet is to create that invisible connection, and to allow the fly to float without drag.

Leaders for the Searching Dry Fly: Searching dries are normally fished over the rougher parts of a stream. The flies are typically large, with a fair amount of wind resistance. Your leader needs to be relatively stout to turn them over. The leader does not need to be very long; trout will not be disturbed by your line tip on wrinkled water. The searching leader should be 8 to 10 feet long, tapered to a tippet of .008" to .006" (3X to 5X). The tippet itself should be about two feet long.

Leaders for Presentation Fishing: When fishing in selective situations, you'll be casting much smaller flies, over smoother water. Your leader needs to be longer, and tapered down to a finer tippet. The presentation leader should be 10 to 15 feet long, tapered to a tippet of .006" to .004" (5X to 7X). The tippet should be 2 to 4 feet long. One of the major causes for refusals when fishing over wary trout is a tippet that has gotten too short through constant changing of flies. Snip off your old tippet and tie on a new one if it gets shorter than about two feet.

Leader Procedure: Nail-knot a permanent one foot butt section to your line tip, using 20 to 25 pound test monofilament. When you change leaders, you no longer have to knot the new one to your line tip each time. Carry a few 7-1/2 and 10 foot store-bought leaders in 3X or 4X. By adding tippet, chosen to suit the situation you encounter, you're always prepared for a variety of conditions. Carry spare tippet spools in .008" (3X), .007" (4X), .006" (5X), and .005" (6X). This allows you to tailor your tippet section to whatever is happening.

Leader Hints: Always buy your basic 7-1/2 and 10 foot leaders and your spare tippet spools in the same brand. Different brands do not hold knots well when joined. Avoid cheap leaders; they have poor tapers. For searching fishing, use a stiff brand of tippet for crisp casting. For presentation fishing, use a limp brand for delicate descents and drag-free floats.

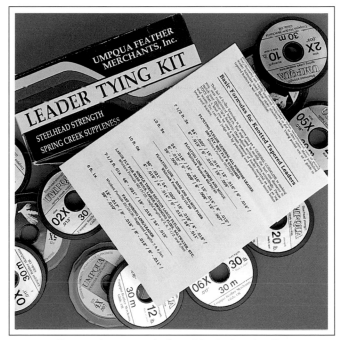

You can tie your own leaders with a leader tying kit.

Proper Diameter, "X", and Fly Size

Dia.	"X"	Fly Size	Dia.	"X"	Fly Size
.011"	0X	1/0, 1, 2	.006"	5X	14, 16, 18, 20
.010"	1X	4, 6, 8	.005"	6X	18, 20, 22, 24
.009"	2X	6, 8, 10	.004"	7X	20, 22, 24, 26
.008"	3X	10, 12, 14	.003"	8X	22, 24, 26, 28
.007"	4X	12, 14, 16			

Note: Tippet strength varies dramatically from brand to brand, so it's best to choose your tippet based on diameter, not pound test. The "X" system is an old way to standardize leader diameters. It is still used so often that it's wise to learn it.

Dry Fly Knots

You need just a few basic knots to be successful in dry fly fishing. The reel knot attaches your backing line to the reel. The nail knot ties backing to the rear of your fly line and a leader butt to the front of it. The surgeon's knot and barrel knot are two ways to tie leader sections together when rebuilding a leader or adding a tippet. The improved clinch knot fixes the fly to your tippet so you can step into the water and catch some trout. Practice each knot at home until you can tie it without trouble or thought.

Reel Knot
(this is the simple Slip Knot)

Step 1: Tie an overhand knot in the tip end of the backing line. Draw it down tight. This keeps the knot from slipping.

Step 2: Run the backing tip around the reel spindle and bring it out five to six inches.

Step 3: Tie an overhand knot around the running part of the backing with the tip of the backing. Draw it down tight and then snug it against the spindle.

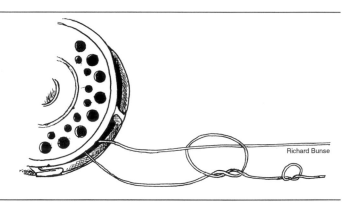

Richard Bunse

Nail Knot
(named because it was originally tied using a nail)

Step 1: Lay a hollow plastic straw, or a nail knot tying tool, alongside your line tip. Overlap five to six inches of backing line or leader butt alongside the line tip and straw.

Step 2: Hold the overlap firmly with the forefinger and thumb of your left hand. Make five to six adjacent wraps of the backing or leader butt around the straw, the line tip, and the running portion of the material being tied on.

Step 3: Insert the tip of the backing or leader butt into the straw, and draw it out the other end. Pull it snug.

Step 4: Pinch your fingers over the wraps and pull the running end of the backing or leader butt snug, tightening the wraps trapped under your fingers.

Step 5: Keep the knot trapped firmly and draw the straw slowly out of the knot. Now pull both ends of the backing or leader butt firmly in opposite directions to seat the wraps tightly around the line tip. Clip the tag ends of line tip and backing or leader butt. Test this and all knots before fishing.

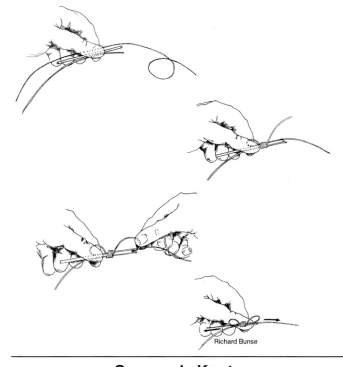

Richard Bunse

Surgeon's Knot

Step 1: Overlap two sections of leader material about four to five inches.

Step 2: Take a simple overhand knot with the overlapped sections, and draw the ends through.

Step 3: Repeat the above with another overhand knot.

Step 4: Moisten the knot with water or saliva, then draw it tight. Clip the ends.

Note: this knot is excellent for joining two sections of leader that are more than .002" different in diameter. The barrel knot does not hold disparate sections as well.

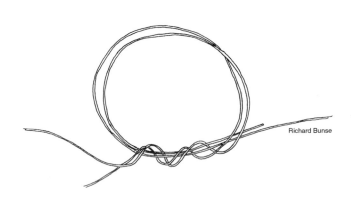

Richard Bunse

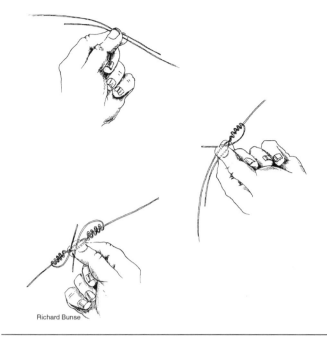

Richard Bunse

Barrel Knot

Step 1: Overlap two ends of leader material five to six inches. Pinch at midpoint of overlap between left thumb and forefinger.

Step 2: Use right thumb and forefinger to wrap right tag end five times around right running end. Reverse the tag end and poke it through the gap formed by the first wrap.

Step 3: Pinch midpoint of overlap and the first five wraps between right thumb and forefinger. Use your left thumb and forefinger to wrap the remaining tag end five times around the running end. Reverse this tag and poke it through the same gap as the first tag end, in the opposite direction.

Step 4: Moisten the knot with water or saliva. Draw the running ends outward slowly but firmly to seat the knot. Clip the tag ends.

Note: this is the tippet knot of choice when the leader sections are close in diameter. If they are not, or if the light is low, use the easier surgeon's knot.

Improved Clinch Knot

Step 1: Hold the fly in your left hand. With your right, run the tippet end through the eye of the fly, and draw it out four to five inches.

Step 2: Take five wraps of the tag end around the running end.

Step 3: Poke the end of the leader through the gap formed by the first wrap next to the hook eye. Draw it all the way through and poke the end through the loop formed by the tag end on one side and the wraps on the other.

Step 4: Moisten the knot with water or saliva. Draw it down, seating the wraps firmly against the eye of the hook. Clip the tag end.

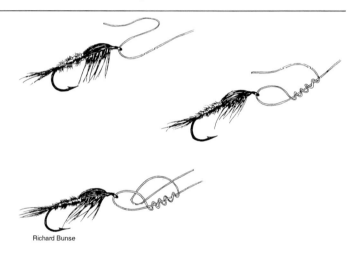

Richard Bunse

Practice tying the right knots well, and you won't break off on trout like this.

Dry Fly Vests and Peripheral Equipment

The right dry fly vest has enough pockets to hold two to four full size fly boxes, plus all of the accessories that make your day on the stream or lake successful and pleasant. Choose your vest for the number and convenient arrangement of its pockets. Make sure they can be securely closed with Velcro or zippers. The vest should have a game pocket in back to hold a rain jacket, wading chains, and water bottle.

Vests come in several lengths. The best is mid-length, with lots of pockets. Full length vests dangle your fly boxes in the water whenever you wade deep. Shorty vests are all right, but rarely hold all that you need. Be sure, when purchasing a vest, that it will fit when stuffed. If it's snug when empty, it will squeeze you like a boa constrictor once you load it.

Fly Boxes: The best dry fly boxes have open compartments, not springs or clips or foam to hold flies. The varieties are endless; some even have individual lids for each separate compartment, so that only one is open at any time. Standard lidded boxes with large compartments are fine. Separate your flies in them by kind and size. Don't stuff the compartments so full that hackles get crushed.

Full size fly boxes, with eight to 10 compartments, are best. It's handy to have one or two tiny boxes, too, for the smallest flies. Some of these have six small lidded compartments. You can use them to hold all the flies you might use for a specific hatch, say ants or little olive mayflies.

Begin with a single large box that holds a selection of searching dries. Later, add another box of patterns that work during specific hatches. As your list of successful dressings builds, your vest might begin to bulge with fly boxes. Keep them as organized as possible, but don't complain: it's an increase in your options, and assures you'll catch fish more often.

Mandatory Supplies: Your vest should always hold the basic leaders and tippet spools already mentioned, plus a pair of leader nippers on a pin-on retractor, dry fly floatant, line cleaner, a hemostat to release your fish, and a handkerchief to clean your hands and fly after you've caught a fish.

Optional Equipment: Your vest should hold a few things you might need astream: sunglasses, sunscreen, bug dope, toilet paper, hook hone, stream thermometer, and a cigarette lighter to start a fire if you take a spill, all in pockets. Add wading chains, water bottle, and a rain jacket to the back compartment.

The author's vest with most of what he carries inside it.

Collecting Equipment: If you observe hatches over the years, and select flies that look a lot like them, you'll up your catch, and also increase the pleasure you get out of each day spent fishing dry flies. A few items will help you observe the insects: a small white jar lid to study trout stomach samples, a magnifying glass, tweezers, an aquarium net, a few vials filled with 70 percent ethyl alcohol, and a pencil and notepad to record your findings.

A few small items—aquarium net, jar lid, magnifying glass, tweezers and vials—let you collect and observe the insects that trout eat.

Waders and Wading

Wader Types: If you're going to have only one set of waders, they should be stocking-foot Neoprenes. Worn with wading boots, these are best when the water has any nip to it. They keep you warm, and are also buoyant. If you fall in they will help you float to safety. Boot-foot Neoprenes, with roomy hip boot feet, are best for extreme cold water.

Thin and light stocking-foot lightweight waders are excellent in warm water. With sufficient pile or wool long underwear, they'll serve through most of the fishing season. They are comfortable, and less tiring, but they are not buoyant like Neoprenes.

Whatever waders you choose, always wear pile underwear or sweat pants under them. Don't wear jeans, cords, or khakis. These stick to the waders, bind you up, tire you out.

Stocking foot (left) and boot foot Neoprene waders are best whenever the water is at all cold.

Hip boots (left) and lightweight waders are excellent options on small streams, or in warm water.

Wading Boots: Choose sturdy wading boots to protect your feet from rocks. The boots should lace high enough to keep out gravel. Add gravel guards or wool stockings outside your waders to prevent chafing and early wear. If the stream bottoms you wade most often are vegetated and slick, felts with tire studs added offer far more traction. If you fish a variety of streams, buy felted wading boots, then carry ice chains or studded sandals to wear over the felts on the slickest streams.

When you buy waders and wading shoes, be sure they fit with all the socks you'll be wearing astream.

Wading Safety: Always wear a belt cinched loosely around the waist of your waders, to keep them from filling if you fall in. When wading water that is neither deep nor dangerous, be sure that one foot is planted before stepping out with the other. When wading dangerous water, consider yourself a three-legged animal: the third leg is your wading staff. Plant it upstream. Be sure that two of your props are always on firm footing. Probe for the next foothold with the other foot or with your staff.

Always keep an eye downstream, and watch where a strong current wants to push you. If it looks dangerous down there, back out before you are unable to wade upstream against the current. Always watch for sloped gravel or mud bars and abrupt edges that might give away beneath you and pitch you into deep water. If you do go in, don't panic. Backpaddle with your hands to keep your head upstream, and use your feet to fend off rocks until you reach water where you can wade again.

Chapter 3

Dry Fly Selection

When pondering what fly to select upon arrival at a stream, or even a lake or pond, divide your thinking into attractor dry flies for searching situations, and imitative dry flies for selective situations. Make a few streamside observations before choosing between the two. Observation reinforces experience. A small body of experience, built over the days, the weeks, and finally over the seasons, will make your dry fly selection accurate and almost automatic.

You'll want to use attractor dries when observation reveals nothing specific going on astream. Trout might be rising, but sporadically, with no rhythm to their rises. Insects might be out, hiding in streamside foliage or even dancing over the water. You'll see a variety of them, not a single dominant species. That's the perfect time for attractor dries. You'll use them most often on the slightly rough water of riffles and runs.

Use imitative patterns when trout hold stations and rise consistently. You'll observe that one or two insect species predominate. You might have to peer closely, nearly touching the water with your nose, or even get out your aquarium net, before you discover what insect prompts trout to feed so selectively. Imitative dries are used most often on smooth runs and flats.

Attractor Dries

The three keys to a successful attractor dry fly are bugginess, flotation and visibility.

Bugginess comes from some resemblance to the foods that trout eat. For example, the Royal Wulff has a mayfly shape, and also has a banded body that looks like a lot of natural insects when it's on the water. The Elk Hair Caddis has a caddisfly shape, and resembles any of the dozens of species of those active insects. The Stimulator imitates a golden stonefly, but it also looks like a caddis or grasshopper awash on the water.

Flotation comes from the use of stiff and water repellant materials. Bodies should be fur from water animals such as muskrat or beaver, or a synthetic. Tails should be stiff hackle fibers or hair. Wings should be hollow hairs from deer or elk, or fluffy stuff like calftail or a synthetic. Hackles should be stiff rooster to make the fly prance on the water.

Visibility is usually added to the wings. White calftail is most common. Bright yellow Polypro yarn wings stand out against all natural colors, are easy to pick out on the water in any light, and do not seem to frighten fish.

Attractor dry flies.

When fishing any attractor dry, coat it well with floatant, then dry it, before making your first cast. Be sure to clean and dress it often to keep it floating high. Whenever it begins to sink on every cast, dry it with your handkerchief, then coat it with floatant again. Before casting, use your handkerchief to remove excess floatant. Then blow vigorously on the fly to fluff all of its fibers. This will make it float better, and also make it look more alive.

Typical water for attractor dry flies.

Imitative Dry Flies

You won't have any trouble deciding when it's time to select an imitative dry. Trout will be rising, and they'll be refusing your attractor dressings. If you're normal, you'll be frustrated. If your fly boxes are normal, they will not contain what you need to imitate every hatch you encounter. Over the years, as your experience with the hatches grows, you'll develop a small list of imitative dries that match the hatches you fish on your own favorite waters.

*Caddisfly adult
and its imitation.*

*Mayfly dun
and its imitation.*

The first step, when encountering a situation where trout are selective, is to do whatever you can to get a look at what they're eating. Use your hat or your aquarium net to catch one. Examine the specimen closely, and recall that trout always see

an insect from the underside in the instant before eating it. That's the side you've got to match.

You don't need to identify an insect to successfully imitate it. All you've got to do is observe its size, shape, and color. Then select the pattern that comes closest to those three features. Get the size right first, the shape as near as you can second. Worry about color last. You'll be surprised how often the wrong fly works so long as it's the right size.

Imitative dry flies are not often fished on rough water. Flotation and visibility are not big problems. As you build a list of dressings for specific hatches, concentrate on the shape of the natural, and choose pattern styles that have the correct silhouette. Many proven patterns are offered in the fly plates in Chapter 8 of this book. They work on hatches spread all across the continent.

Smooth water, where you would expect to need exact imitations.

Chapter 4

Dry Fly Casting

All dry fly presentations are built on the same basic fly cast. You simply modify it to make all sorts of presentation casts. Twenty to 40 foot casts catch most trout on dry flies. Don't go for distance in the beginning. Instead, practice for delicacy and precision.

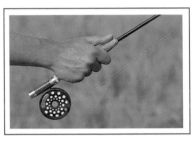

The basic cast is broken into just two parts: the backcast and forecast. Each fore- and backcast is made up of three rod movements: the load, power and drift. It's easy to memorize. With a little practice, it's also easy to execute. Begin with the proper rod grip, cradling the fingers loosely around the cork, and aligning the thumb precisely on the top of the grip.

Proper Backcast: Begin with the line stretched out 20-30 feet on the lawn. Point the rod straight down the line. Load the backcast by lifting the rod smoothly to the one o'clock position on an imaginary clock face, moving your forearm but keeping your wrist straight. This starts the line in motion and sets its weight against the rod tip.

Continue into the power stroke without pause, by driving the rod sharply through the short arc between 1:00 and 12:00. Use the strength of your forearm, shoulder, and wrist in this fast, strong stroke. Stop the rod abruptly as near to straight overhead as you can.

Let the rod drift without power, to the 10:00 o'clock position behind you. The largest mistake made in fly casting is forgetting this stop, so that the rod continues to power the line down through the drift part of the backcast. This merely drills the line into the ground. When fishing, you'll catch grass or brush or whatever else lurks behind you.

Proper Forecast: When the line has straightened in the air behind you, at rod tip height and parallel to the ground, begin your forecast. Load the rod with a forearm movement and straight wrist, pushing the rod smoothly from 10:00 to 11:00. This takes slack out of the line, and sets its weight against the rod tip.

Apply the power stroke from 11:00 to 12:00, using the strength and speed of your forearm, shoulder, and wrist. Stop the rod nearly straight overhead. Recall that the largest mistake made in fly casting is to power the rod too far and drive the line toward the ground on both fore- and backcasts.

Let the rod drift without power from 12:00 down to 2:00, while the line straightens in the air. When it is straight you are ready to begin the same cycle for the next backcast: load, power and drift. The basic cast is a series of forecasts and backcasts followed by a delivery stroke that drops the fly to the water.

Proper backcast

Proper forecast

Extending the Cast: While the line straightens in the air on each forecast, let a few feet of line slip through you fingers to lengthen the cast. Don't do this until you've mastered the basic fore- and backcast with 20 to 30 feet of line in the air.

The Casting Plain: The normal forecast and backcast travel parallel to the ground. When your load, power, and drift are all timed correctly, the line will travel at rod tip height in front and in back, never scorching the ground in either direction.

The Delivery Stroke: In dry fly fishing, accuracy and delicacy are very important. You achieve these on the delivery stroke: the final forecast that places the fly on the water precisely where you want it.

For accuracy, aim the rod at the exact point where you want the fly to land. The line always follows the direction of the rod tip. To get the distance right, measure it on the next-to-last forecast. That is what forecasts are for: to extend line, measure the range, and refine your aim.

On the delivery stroke, aim the final forecast at a point about waist high above the water. Let the rod tip drift down to that same height. The line loop will unfold, the leader will turn over, and the fly will float gently down right where you want it.

If you aim the delivery stroke too low, the line will smash into the water, frightening fish. If you aim it too high, the leader will tower straight into the air, then land in a pile.

The Roll Cast: The roll cast is excellent where you're hemmed in by brush, and lack room for a backcast. It rolls line out in front without the need to sail it into danger behind you. The roll cast requires water tension to load the rod; you can't practice this one on a lawn.

Begin the roll cast with a few feet of line stripped from the reel and piled onto the water beyond the rod tip. Lift the rod and bring the tip back over your shoulder to 1:00, the position for beginning the proper power stroke in the basic cast. The line will slide across the water toward the rod.

Just as the line slides far enough to settle into a slight curve behind the rod, put on a sharp power stroke to 12:00, then stop the power abruptly. The rod will drift through 12:00. But if you power it much past that, the line will fail to roll out in a tight ball. The cast will pile up rather than turning over.

Repeat two or three rolls to extend the line out to where you want to fish your dry fly. With some practice you'll be able to fish 30 to 40 feet away using the roll cast. Most often it's used in tight situations, at 20 to 30 feet.

Correct position of the rod and line at beginning of roll cast.

Stop the rod high and the line will roll out in a tight loop.

Drag and the Dry Fly

In his classic 1938 book *Trout*, Ray Bergman called "...that old devil drag" the dry fly fisherman's worst enemy. He wasn't wrong then. The most modern rods, lines, and leaders still fail to solve drag unless you are careful to use them properly.

Drag is any unnatural movement of your dry fly when it's on the water. A natural insect drifts without any hindrence from a line or leader. If your dry fly does not appear to drift the same way, trout will notice the difference and shy away. Even a perfect imitation will not fool any trout if the fly drags, and therefore does not act like a natural.

A dragging fly will turn trout away.

Causes of Drag: Conflicting currents are the most common cause of drag. Whenever you cast across two or more currents that move at different speeds, or in different directions, the line and leader get pulled straight, and the fly begins to scoot. Drag can be caused by a leader tippet that is too stiff for the size fly, or a tippet that is too short. Both cause the leader to tug the fly across the surface.

If you overpower the delivery stroke, the leader will land too straight on the water, causing drag. The proper delivery stroke is soft and aimed at the right height: the leader turns over, then drifts down to the water. It lands with some slack in it, allowing the fly its freedom. Another casting problem is the cross-stream or downstream cast made without any slack. The current straightens the leader instantly, and the fly cuts a V-wake on top.

Most of the time drag is barely visible to you, or even invisible, from your distant casting position. Trout get a close view. They notice drag that escapes you. Always be aware of drag, and try to solve it whenever you fail to fool fish.

Solutions to Drag: The first step is to be sure that your tippet is at least two feet long, and fine enough for the size fly you're using (See chart on page 11).

The next step is to observe the water carefully and take up a casting position that has most conflicting currents behind you, not between you and the lie to which you wish to cast. Position yourself to cast quartering upstream wherever you can, so that the fly drifts downstream toward you, without influence from the line or leader.

The final step is to adjust your casting to compensate for drag. Read the currents carefully, gauge what they'll do to your leader and fly, then use the presentation that will give you a drag-free drift. Cast softly so the leader does not land straight. If you must cast across stream, use the Reach Cast. If you must cast downstream, use the Wiggle Cast. These, and most other casts described in the rest of this chapter, are designed to help you prevent drag in specific situations.

Conflicting currents cause most unseen drag.

Good Drag: Drag used right can help you entice fish to your dry fly. It usually works best when insects such as caddis are out, dancing over the water and dapping their eggs on the surface. Try casting downstream with a short line. Let the fly float a bit, then tug it just a few inches upstream. Let it drift again. Hop and skitter it on the surface. Whenever trout refuse your dry on the drag-free drift, try giving the fly some animation. It might prompt trout into striking.

Intentional drag can attract trout.

Fishing the Dry Fly Upstream

The upstream cast is the standard dry fly technique. It lets you approach from downstream, behind the prying eyes of the trout: they always hold facing into the current. It also helps solve drag, because the fly drifts downstream toward the rod, building slack in the line and leader.

The upstream cast is most effective on rough water: riffles, runs, and pocket water. Because line flying overhead frightens trout, the upstream cast is not effective on smooth water unless your leader is very long.

Wherever possible, avoid casting straight upstream. That sends the line and leader right over the drift line the fly will follow: right over the heads of the trout you hope to catch. Instead, cast at an angle quartering upstream and across the current. Then the line and leader soar through the air off to the side of the drift line. They also remain off to the side during the drift. The cast quartering up and across, rather than straight upstream, can make the difference between lots of trout and no trout at all. The quartering cast also allows you to fish the upstream dry on smooth water, over wary trout.

Handling Slack Line: With the upstream dry, your line moves downstream toward you as the drift unfolds, creating slack. You must control this slack in order to set the hook when a fish hits. Drape the line over the forefinger of your casting hand, beneath the rod grip. Then draw slack over that finger with your line hand. Pull just fast enough to keep ahead of the drift, without moving the fly. On slow water, ease line in. On fast water, strip line like crazy.

Wherever possible, make your upstream casts quartering across the current.

Patterning the Water: You'll fish the upstream dry most often where it's difficult to see trout or pinpoint their lies. In a riffle or run of even depth and current speed, trout are usually sprinkled wherever rocks of the right size break the flow along the bottom. It's best to pattern the water to cover all of these scattered lies.

Start at the lower end of the riffle or run. Make your first cast short, and nearly straight upstream. Cover the water with a series of drifts that parallel each other one to three feet apart, working across the holding water. Make the second series of parallel drifts about a leader length higher up in the current. That way you cast over trout that haven't seen the line time after time. The fly is a surprise to them.

When you've covered all of the water you can reach from the first position, wade upstream a few feet and begin the process again. Pattern the water as you move upstream, and you'll spend your entire day casting over undisturbed fish.

On water where trout could hold anywhere, be sure to cover all potential lies. Set up a disciplined casting pattern, and cover all of the water with a series of parallel dry fly drifts. Move to a new position only after you've covered all of the water you can reach from the first casting position.

Fishing Holding Lies with the Upstream Dry: Some holding lies are obvious. Trout hold both above and below rocks breaking the current. They hold along ledges, and down on the bottom in trenches. They crouch beneath undercut banks. These are all obvious lies.

Many types of lies are described in Chapter 5. But experience is always your best teacher. Whenever you catch a trout, take note of the water from which it arose. You'll find other trout in similar places as you move up and down the stream you're on, and as you move from stream to stream.

Never charge right to a lie. You'll spook fish holding near-by, and they'll frighten those in the lie. Ease up to an obvious lie in the course of patterning the water around it. Then fish the best water with several extra casts, from the shortest range possible. Crowd your drifts together over the obvious lie. Repeat each float two or three times, tempting the trout with more chances to see the fly and rush to the top.

If the lie is a boulder protruding from the surface, the water pillowing against it on the upstream side forms a soft lie at least as good as the lie downstream from it. Many people fish below a boulder, then reel up and leave it without fishing just above it, where half the trout hold.

Approach an obvious holding lie, such as the slick behind the big boulder, very cautiously. Fish your way to it so you do not frighten other fish, which will spook those in the sweet spot. Use the up-and-across cast to fish the lie thoroughly.

The Reach Cast

Often you'll find yourself fishing smooth water, over wary trout, where a cross-stream cast is far more effective than the upstream dry. The smooth currents your line cuts across often conflict, though sometimes they'll be a single sheet. Either way, if you cast a straight line across stream to the precise point where you want the fly to land, you'll get just two to three feet of free drift before the line comes tight. Then you've got drag. The reach cast allows you to cast across stream and still get a five to 15 foot drift without drag.

Making the Reach Cast: Take up your position across stream from the lie you want to fish, or from visible and rising trout. Get as close as you can. The reach cast is most effective at 20 to 40 feet. If you're within 25 feet of rising trout, crouch to keep your profile low, and tilt your rod to the side.

To execute the reach cast, drive the rod forward in a normal power stroke. Aim it exactly at the point where you want the fly to land. As the rod drifts down into the waist-high position of the delivery stroke, tip it over to the upstream side. While the line still travels in the air, reach out as far as you can with the rod and with your arm. The fly will land where you aimed it, but the line will land at an angle across the current, upstream from the fly.

Following the Drift: As the fly begins its drift, follow it downstream with the rod tip. This is the core of the reach cast: the line and leader, upstream from the fly, follow it down apace, and let it float without drag. If the current near you is faster than that out near the fly, hold the rod high to lift the line off the water. If necessary, flick mends down the back of the line to keep it following the fly (see Mending Line, page 29).

Completing the Drift: As the drift continues, the fly will reach a position straight across from you. Your rod should be pointed nearly straight at the fly. To extend the float as far as possible, reach downstream with the rod and follow the fly. Continue to reach downstream until the line comes tight and the fly begins to drag. Then pick up and make another reach cast.

The proper reach cast lands on the water with the line lying upstream from the fly. Your rod and arm should be stretched out as far as possible.

As the fly drifts downstream, follow it with the rod tip. This allows the fly a long drift free of any drag. Move your rod and arm at the same pace as the fly and the line. Throughout most of the drift, point the rod right down the line at the fly.

To extend the drag-free drift of the dry fly, in the reach cast, follow with the rod after the fly passes directly in front of you. The farther you can reach downstream with the rod and your arm, the longer the effective drift you'll get.

The Downstream Wiggle Cast

At times you can find the right fly, and present it carefully to rising trout with an upstream cast or reach cast, but still fail to fool the fish. Then it's wise to find a casting position that allows you to show the fly to the fish first, drifting downstream ahead of the line and leader. That means you must cast from upstream. A cast downstream with a straight line would cause instant drag.

You can solve these situations with the downstream wiggle cast. It's amazing how often this cast lets you suddenly begin catching trout that were impossible with all other presentations.

Position for the Wiggle Cast: Correct position is nearly as important as execution with this cast. Slip into the water upstream from a feeding fish without sending wading waves down over it. Waves put trout down. Move very slowly, and edge within 25 to 35 feet of the fish, not straight upstream, but at a 20 to 40 degree angle off to the side. This allows you to lift your fly for the next cast without disturbing the fish if it refuses your first few drifts.

Executing the Wiggle Cast: When preparing to make the cast, first get the right amount of line in the air to make a presentation directly to the fish, plus an extra 10 feet or so. Make these measuring forecasts off to the side, so the line in the air doesn't go over the fish and put it down.

Aim your delivery stroke at the point where you want the fly to land. This will usually be three to five feet upstream from the feeding fish. Selective trout rarely move far out of a feeding lane to take an insect, or a dry fly. You've got to set the fly on the water almost precisely in the line of drift that leads to the trout's occasionally arising nose.

As the line unfurls in the air, wobble your rod from side to side. Do this as you drop the rod to the waist-high position of the delivery stroke. This wobbling will send a series of S-turns down the line. The line will land on the water like a snake out for a swim. As the S-curves straighten out, the fly is allowed a free drift downstream. It arrives over the fish ahead of the line and leader. The fly is the first thing the trout sees.

If the trout does not take, let the fly drift past it. Tilt the rod and let the current draw the fly to the side. To avoid spooking the fish, lift the fly for the next cast only after it has been drawn far enough away. That's why you take your position slightly to the side, not straight upstream.

> **Adding Wiggle to an Upstream Cast or Reach Cast:** Whenever you fish smooth water with an upstream cast or reach cast, invisible drag can cause refusals that you can't explain. Try adding some wiggle to your normal casts. You'll be surprised how often you suddenly begin fooling the fish. It's because your fly is getting a free drift out there, without some slight drag that trout can see, but you can't.

Before making the downstream wiggle cast, work your way carefully into the right position, upstream from feeding fish. Take your position slightly off to the side, never directly upstream, so that you're not forced to cast straight downstream. Work your line out, and measure your cast carefully, before making the back-cast and forecast.

When you've done the downstream wiggle cast correctly, the fly should land just two or three feet above the position of the rising trout. Always place the fly in a direct line above the trout, not off to the side. The line should land in a series of S-curves. These will feed the fly downstream to the waiting trout, without drag.

The Parachute Cast

The parachute cast is another way to get a drag-free drift while casting downstream. It can be used in place of the wiggle cast, but is not so accurate, and therefore not as effective when you've got a single rising trout pinpointed. It's best for lies like boulders, and for situations where you want to use cast after cast to pattern the water while fishing downstream.

The parachute cast is useful even in rough riffles and runs if they are heavily fished. It's a way to present the fly ahead of the line and leader. That's different from what the trout see all day long from other fishermen. Often that difference is enough to let you fool the fish.

The Parachute Cast: Wade into position to fish at an angle downstream, 25 to 40 feet from the water you want to cover. Make normal forecasts and backcasts, based on the basic cast, but work 10 to 20 feet of extra line in the air. Use a normal but slightly overpowered delivery stroke. Stop it at 12:00, with the rod straight overhead, just as you always would. Aim this delivery stroke high, at rod tip level, rather than dropping the rod to waist height as you would on a typical delivery stroke.

The Bounce: Hold the rod high while the line loop straightens in the air. When the line is straight, or nearly so, bounce it back toward you with a slight jerk of the rod. This takes no more than a twitch of your wrist. The straight line will get a jolt in the air, and will recoil into a series of S-curves that settle to the water. End the cast with your rod tip held almost straight up, and your casting arm drawn in tight against your body.

The Follow: The S-curves of line on the water will feed slowly downstream, giving the fly a free and natural drift. As the curves begin to disappear, lower the rod tip, then extend your arm, following the drift and extending it a few more feet. You can also draw slack from the reel and shake your rod from side to side to toss this slack onto the water. It will follow the fly and extend the drift.

You can get 15 to 20 feet of drag-free drift with the parachute cast, but it's better to attempt five to 10 feet, lifting for the next cast before invisible drag sets in.

Patterning the Water: The parachute cast is often best when you're fishing a riffle or run. It's most effective to cover all of such water with a disciplined casting pattern, just as you would with the upstream dry.

Make the first cast straight downstream. Fish out the drift, then lift the fly and place it one to three feet out from the first cast. This will give you a parallel drift. Repeat the process until you've extended your casts outward to cover as much water as you can. Then wade downstream about the length of the drifts you've been getting: 10 feet or so. Start the next series of drifts right where you lifted the fly at the end of the first series of drifts, to cover new water and undisturbed trout.

The parachute cast is exactly like the basic cast, except that the delivery stroke is stopped abruptly, with the rod held nearly straight up. The line will recoil, and land on the water with lots of slack. Keep your casting arm drawn in toward your side, and hold the rod tip up.

As the fly drifts downstream toward the lie of the trout, in the parachute cast, the slack in the line will pay out, giving the fly a free drift. To extend the drift, lower your rod tip slowly, and reach out with your rod arm as far as you can. To make your pickup for the next cast, tilt the rod and let the current draw the line off to the side before lifting it.

The Sidearm Cast

The sidearm cast lets you tip the rod over and lay the casting loop on its side. The casting loop unfurls parallel to the water and just above it. This cast will slip your fly beneath branches and into places you could never reach without it. It's most useful on tree-lined streams.

The sidearm cast is also valuable on spring creek flats, or when you wade the shallows of a lake, casting to visible cruisers. At anything less than about 25 feet, they can see your rod movement when you cast. Solution: tip the rod to the side so it's below the trouts' line of sight.

The sidearm cast is nothing more than the basic fly cast tipped on its side. Tilt the rod anywhere from shoulder to hip height. Stoop if you need to, which you often will. Keep the cast short and use brisk fore- and backcasts: load, power, and drift. The drift phase must be shortened: the line will drop to the water if you pause too long.

Off-shoulder and Off-hand Casting: If you get into a tree-shrouded situation that does not allow a normal cast, you might be able to cast off-shoulder. Reach your casting arm across your chest. Tilt the rod away from whatever obstructs it. Your normal forecasts and backcasts will be shortened, but you'll be able to cast a fair distance, and cover water you could not otherwise reach.

In many situations it helps if you learn to cast with the off hand. For example, if you're right-handed and fishing upstream along the right bank of a tree-shrouded stream, switch and cast with your left hand. Don't try to cast long; short casts are all you need in such situations, anyway.

Don't switch to the off hand in difficult situations at first. Just try it for a few casts at times whenever fishing is slow. You'll be surprised how quickly you learn to deliver the fly at 25 to 35 feet. Then you've acquired a new way to tackle tough spots. The more options you've got, the more fish you can catch.

The sidearm cast lets you slip your fly up under brush. You could not place your fly into some of the most promising lies with the basic overhand cast.

Learn to cast from the off-shoulder, and through the years, practice casting with your off-hand. This will allow you to fish places where trees or brush behind you might snare an errant backcast.

Right and Left Curve Casts

Once you've learned the sidearm cast, then you can easily hook your leader around to the left, or drop it softly off to the right, to clear obstacles such as midstream or bankside boulders. Curve casts are also great when you must approach a rising trout, or suspected lie, from downstream, but don't want to put your line or leader over it. Curves allow you to float the fly down the trout's feeding lane while keeping the line and leader off to the side. (If you're not right-handed, the following casts are the same but the direction of the curves are opposite.)

Left Curve Cast: To execute the left curve, make a normal sidearm cast, but overpower the delivery stroke and aim it slightly high. The extra power causes the line tip and leader to hook around in a curve to the left. This cast requires a properly proportioned leader. If it is too long and limp, the curve will fail to form.

Right Curve Cast: To make a right curve, tip the rod into a sidearm cast, and underpower the delivery stroke. The line loop does not unfurl completely. The line tip and leader land on the water hooked around to the right. This cast is difficult to make work more than 50 percent of the time, even for experts. It can help you catch trout you would not have a chance at without it.

Roll Cast Pickup: If you lift the fly for the next cast by pulling it straight toward the rod, water tension on the line and leader can cause the line to rip off the water, spooking fish. You can avoid this with the roll cast pickup. It is useful in any situation where you want a delicate liftoff.

To execute the roll cast pickup, merely flick a loop down the line, using the roll cast movement described on page 19. When the loop reaches the line tip and leader, it will lift them into the air. Start your backcast at that moment, and it will cause no disturbance. The roll cast pickup is effective only at short range, out to about 35 to 40 feet.

The Steeple Cast

Often the best position for a cast backs you up against tall grass or brush. The roll cast is one solution. It disturbs the water less to use a steeple cast to clear the obstacle.

Turn to examine your backcast area, gauging how high the line must go to clear what's behind you. You might discover a gap in the grass or trees, and aim the backcast for it. The possibilities become endless, and you become far less restricted, so long as you study what's behind you, and find room for your backcast.

To execute the steeple cast, just tilt the plain of your basic casting stroke down in front, up in back. In the normal cast, the line moves back and forth parallel to the ground, 10 to15 feet above it. In the steeple cast, you drive the backcast high by tilting the casting plain upward. Then turn back to your target and drive the forecast toward the point where you want the fly to land.

Keep the steeple cast short. Don't try for more than one, or at most two, backcasts. The less casting you do, the fewer troubles you'll get into.

In the steeple cast, the backcast is driven high over obstacles behind you.

Position as Part of every Cast

When assessing a potential bit of holding water, an obvious lie, or the pinpoint lie of a rising trout, look for the best position to launch a cast for a drag-free float. Usually one approach is best, and all others will cause problems. For example, you might find a lie surrounded by a seething of conflicting currents that will kill a cast from downstream, or from either side. That leaves the approach from upstream the only one that will work. You've got to move in and make your cast from that direction for the best chance to catch a fish.

When moving into the chosen position, be sure you do not send any wading waves over the water you want to fish. Once you've sent disturbing waves over fish, they're either gone, or they're put on edge and are not likely to take a dry. Careless wading costs far more trout than fishermen ever find out about.

When you've chosen the best position, waded to it, and are ready to make the cast, make sure you're out of sight of the trout. If they see you, they're gone. The closer you get, the lower you've got to stoop. If you're on shore and within 15 to 20 feet of the fish, crouch or get down on hands and knees. If you're wading that close, stoop and make a sidearm cast to keep the rod out of the trout's line of sight.

Mending Line

Most line control problems should be solved before your line lands on the water. Choose your casting position carefully, then use the basic cast, roll cast, reach cast, wiggle cast, or a combination of a couple of the casts. Do whatever it takes to create a drag-free drift.

Often currents conflict in such a way that they push a belly into the line after it's on the water, tightening the line and causing drag. A belly forms when the current near the fly is either faster or slower than that close to you. A downstream belly is caused by faster currents near you. An upstream belly, less common, is caused by faster currents out in the drift lane.

You can take care of either kind of belly with an upstream or downstream mend. Most often, the line belly will form downstream, and you'll want an upstream mend. Do it before the fly begins to drag. The goal is to flip the belly over and upstream without moving the fly. The longer you wait, the tighter the line, and the less chance you can mend successfully.

Execution of the Mend: For an upstream mend, lower your rod almost to the water, and reach the tip downstream. Flick the rod up and over in a quick rolling motion in front of your body. This lifts the line off the water and loops it over upstream. The rod should end low to the water and reaching upstream. The downstream line belly will lift off the water, roll over in the air, and land in an upstream belly. For a less common downstream mend, lay the rod over upstream, then roll it up and over to toss the belly downstream.

Mend when a downstream belly forms in line, before it causes drag.

Roll the rod briskly up and over, lifting the line.

The line will land on water in an upstream belly, eliminating drag.

Often it's necessary to mend two or three times on the same drift. Some drifts require a series of constant mends to keep the fly from dragging. Be creative; respond to what the line tells you needs to be done.

Setting the Hook

Trout in fast water must make quick decisions, and normally take dry flies on the dash. When you fish riffles, rough runs, and pocket water, set the hook quickly. Keep all slack out of the line as the fly floats toward you. Raise the rod swiftly and set the hook vigorously, though not any harder than your leader tippet will withstand without snapping.

When you fish slow or still water, usually with imitative flies over trout that are sipping and selective, takes will be slow, almost thoughtful. Set the hook patiently. Your tippet will be much finer. The fine point of a small hook doesn't need to be driven home, anyway. In such situations, set the hook with a slow and gentle lifting of the rod.

Small fish smack dries without doubt. You can set the hook on them instantly. A big trout accepts a dry fly with a sort of ponderousness. You've got to wait until it tips down with the fly before you set the hook, or you'll merely pull the fly away. If you miss a big fish, it will rarely come back.

As a rough rule, set the hook quickly in fast water, slowly and gently in slow water.

Playing Fish

You can play small trout by stripping line with your line hand, using the forefinger of your rod hand to control it. Hold your rod tip high, so the fish runs and tugs against the spring of the full rod.

It's best to play large trout off the reel. Set the hook, then use your line hand to control the line for the first few moments. Draw in any slack quickly; never let the fish run around at the end of a slack line. Once you've got all slack taken in, or more likely once the trout has made a run and taken all the slack out, play the fish directly from the reel. Set the drag loose to protect the tippet. When the fish runs, let the reel give it line. When the fish comes toward you, take up line with the reel.

Again, keep the rod tip high, and let the fish fight this spring. If the trout jumps, lower the rod so the trout does not land against a tight line, which might break the tippet.

Tilting rod tips fish off balance and tires it quickly.

Landing and Releasing Fish

Land trout as quickly as you can to release them full of vigor, when their survival is highest. If you use a net, be sure it has soft cotton meshes, not abrasive nylon. Lead the trout over the lip of the net, then scoop it up. Do not stab at the fish; you'll just knock it off the hook. Remove the fly and get the fish back into the water at once. Never hold a trout out of water for more than half a minute. It will die as surely as you would drown if the trout caught you and held you under water to release you unharmed.

If you land a trout by hand, play it until you can hold its head up out of the water with pressure from the rod. Then lead it over your hand, and support it gently in the water. Remove the hook quickly, and let the fish swim out of your hand. Use your hemostat if you have any trouble removing the hook, which should be barbless.

If a trout has worn itself out, and has difficulty keeping itself upright in the water, don't release it right away. Instead, gently restrain it with one hand under its belly and the other with a light grip around the wrist of its tail. Hold it upright in the water, facing into the current, until it is strong enough to swim out of your hands under its own power.

To photograph a fish, hold it in the water while the photographer sets the light setting and focus. Then lift the trout out of the water just long enough to snap the shot. Settle the fish back to the water and release it as soon as you can.

For a photo keep fish in water, lift it briefly for click.

Chapter 5

Fishing Dry Flies on Moving Water

Certain indicators predict success with dry flies. Their absence does not necessarily mean you'll fail if you fish dries. However, their presence is a prediction that trout will be up and active: willing to strike at flies fished on the surface.

The first indicator is visibly rising trout. If you see fish feeding on the surface, then they're prime for the right dry. If the rises are sporadic, and in fairly fast water, then reach for a high-floating searching dry. If the rises are rhythmic and in fairly smooth water, suspect selectivity, and attempt to find and match whatever the trout are taking.

The next indicator, in the absence of rises, is shallow and somewhat lively water. In water much more than five or six feet deep, trout are not likely to burst up to the surface to take a dry fly. If the water lacks much movement, trout aren't often willing to feed up top without some insect activity to draw them there. In moving water two to four feet deep, however, they're attuned to taking up top, and will rush there eagerly to intercept your fly.

Water temperature is an excellent indicator. If the water is below about 50 degrees, trout are not likely to feed at the surface unless a hatch of insects draws them there. If it's between 55 and 65 degrees, trout will be most interested in the surface. In water above 65 degrees, they start to get lethargic.

The best indications for the dry fly are slightly empirical. You'll learn to recognize them instantly as you acquire experience astream. These include sunshine and enough warmth to rev the motors of insects and trout. When the air and the water are warmed by the sun, and you see insects out and about, trout have a general awareness of the matter. Their attention is drawn upward. They move into positions where they can rise swiftly to the top. In hot spells, it's the opposite: they look toward the top during the cool parts of the day, at dawn and dusk.

When insects are out and about, trout will be on the prod for dry flies.

Fishing Fast and Shallow Water

Shallow water is the most productive because sunlight strikes to the bottom, causes photosynthetic plant growth, which feeds insects, which feed trout. In shallow water, trout constantly look up. In fast water, trout must make quick decisions. Watch awhile and you'll see splashy rises in riffles and shallow runs.

Fish fast and shallow water with short casts up and across the current.

High-floating searching flies are perfect in fast water. Use them in size 10 through 14. They should be buggy to entice the trout, and visible so you can detect takes. The Royal Wulff, Humpy, and Elk Hair Caddis are among the most effective. Always use your own favorites; they will work best for you.

Because the surface is broken, and fish are not able to see so well, your best approach is from downstream. Fish the water with short upstream casts, recalling that it's always best to cast up and across, not straight upstream. Cover all of the water in a disciplined fashion. Make a few extra casts above, below, and to both sides of any obvious lie such as a midstream boulder, ledge, or trench.

In this fast and shallow water, the largest mistake you can make is getting rooted to one spot. Trout will normally take a fly on the first or second drift. If you take up a casting position, and cover all of the water you can reach in a way that shows the fly to all potential lies once or twice, that's enough. Wade up a few feet and begin casting again. If you stand in one spot and pound the water, you're wasting time. Keep moving, moving.

Fishing Pocket Water: Pockets of slow water form in rapids and even cascades wherever the current gets interrupted, usually by a boulder. It's often a trench in the bottom. Trenches in fast water show up as slight slicks, just a few feet long, on the surface.

Because water surrounding pockets is turbulent, you can wade very close to them without disturbing trout. Move to between 15 and 25 feet before making your first cast. The closer you get, the more conflicting currents you have behind you.

Dance your dry fly on the surface of the pocket. Make the short cast, then lift the rod high to loft line and leader off the water. This is dapping: set the fly to the water, let it dance, lift it off, set it down again.

Sometimes an approach from upstream is easier, and at times more effective. Make the cast downstream with a high rod. Lower the rod into the drift to let the fly float down a ways. Then lift it to skitter and hop the fly back upstream. Lower the rod and let the fly drift again. Lots of natural caddis act this way on the water. When a trout hits your dry fished this way, it will be with a detonation.

Fish pocket water with close casts and a high rod.

Fishing the Dry Fly
in Moderate Water

When you fish water of moderate flow and medium depth, say three to six feet, you'll often look for something specific to prompt your casts. It might be a suspected lie, or an obvious lie, or even a trout you've spotted rising. With such a specific target in sight, you then scout the best position to make the cast, and the best approach to move into that position without disturbing the fish.

Never eliminate searching as a strategy on water of moderate depth. Where the water is relatively unfeatured, when no trout rise, you can still draw trout to dries. This is especially true when the indicators stated on page 31 predict success. Trout will be looking up. When conditions are right, set up a disciplined casting pattern to cover all of the water with your favorite searching dry.

The most common case is the stalk of a specific lie, in the course of moving upstream and casting constantly over water with a moderate flow. Such lies should be noted carefully and fished diligently. They include seams where currents of two different speeds merge; boulders or logs or anything else breaking the current; ledges and trenches where the bottom depth is suddenly different from that around it; and any gravel shelves or corner eddies where shallow and fast water rushes into the slower water you're fishing.

You'll often spot rising trout in moderate water. When you do, it's worth taking a couple of careful casts over them with the fly you're using at the moment, especially if it's been taking trout. Don't pound the trout with it. If it's refused a few times, spend a moment trying to find out what the trout are feeding on, then try to find a fly that matches it fairly closely.

In water of moderate depth and current speed, you'll apply all of the casting techniques outlined in Chapter 4. You'll use the upstream cast while searching the water. You'll use the reach cast to fish lies that are best approached from the side. You'll employ the delicate downstream wiggle cast to tempt rising and selective trout. On lots of occasions, you'll need to mend line. At times, you'll use creative combinations of two or three techniques, designed to solve the problem of a drag-free drift to a particular lie, or to a rising trout.

In water of moderate depth and speed, carefully cover all specific lies, such as this boulder.

The Dry Fly in Deep Water

Most of the time, trout hold on the bottom unless something draws them toward the surface. In the absence of active feeding, assume that trout are on the bottom of any piece of

Wade the inside of a bend pool, and cast to the deep outside.

water you approach. In calm, clear water, they might rise six to eight feet to take a dry fly. In rough or cloudy water, the limit is reduced to three or four feet. Trout have an instinct for the balance between energy expended to get something to eat, and the energy gained from getting it. They won't spear up through eight to 10 feet of water for a small dry fly, and often will ignore a large one as well.

Bend pools have their depths pushed to the outside edge, up against the far bank. They're excellent places to fish a dry because trout are used to seeing insects drop in from nearby grasses and bushes. To fish them, wade the shallow inside edge, and cast across the shallows to the main current on the outside. If the far bank is undercut and deep, kiss your searching dry right to it, and cause it to drift along the edge as far as you can.

Narrow bend pools call for up-and-across stream casts. If a pool

is so wide that you can't cast upstream and still reach the far shore, then cast straight across with the reach cast. The current is normally fastest against the far bank, and slowest under your rod. Be prepared to make a long reach, and to do lots of mending, to get a good drift.

Most deep pools have shallow dry fly water at the head and tailout. Fish the head with upstream casts, working far up into the back eddies at the corners, where the shallow water breaks over into the head of the pool.

Fish tailouts with the reach cast. Start at the side nearest you, and drift the fly in the lifting water at the lower end of the pool. You'll get short drifts and drag, even with the reach. If a mend won't take care of it, pick the fly off the water and make the next cast a foot or two farther out. Sometimes you'll have to wade into position upstream and fish tailouts down with the wiggle cast. This works best when trout are active and visibly feeding in the shallows at the foot of a pool.

At times, a skittered fly works well in a tailout, especially when caddisflies dance over the water. Cast downstream toward the tail. Feed line and let the fly drift a few feet. Then lift the rod to hop the fly and skate it upstream a foot or so. Drop the rod and let it drift again. Takes will be against a tight line. Set the hook softly to keep from breaking off.

Fish dries far up into the "corner" of any deep pool.

The Dry Fly on Smooth Water

Trout on flat water usually rise at the surface in response to some particular insect activity. They'll often feed selectively. You've got to respond with fine gear, the right fly, and the correct presentation before you fool them.

Finding fish is the first key to fishing smooth water. You'll usually locate them not by locating potential lies, but by spotting rises. Sometimes they're obvious, but often they're mere pips in the surface film. Train yourself to watch water carefully. It doesn't hurt to carry a pair of small binoculars to watch for rises, and also to spy from long range on what the trout might be taking.

The next step is to get into position. The best position to approach most rising trout is from the side, or from an angle upstream, so you can cast downstream to them. This calls for extremely careful wading on smooth water. Wading waves will put trout down. Be sure to stay out of sight, stooping if necessary when you get in close to the trout.

Fly selection can be critical when fishing over rising trout on smooth water. Most often you'll want to come as close as possible to matching whatever they're taking. It helps to carry a small collecting kit to observe the insects, and to have a small selection of hatch matching flies from which to choose. But you can sometimes modify an existing pattern by nipping off its tails, wings, and whatever to make it look like the real thing.

Presentation is the final element to successful fishing on smooth water. The position you've taken will dictate the cast that you use. Most of the time it will be the cross-stream reach cast or the downstream wiggle cast. Be sure to place the fly on the water as delicately as you can. If you're forced to cast upstream, make sure it's an up-and-across approach, so that your line and leader do not fly over the trout. If you must use an upstream cast, or even a reach cast, try adding an element of wiggle to it, so the leader lands with slack, and you get a drift free of invisible drag.

When fishing smooth water, use your light presentation outfit. Your leader should be 10 to 14 feet long. The tippet should be long and fine. Use the chart on page 11 to choose the right tippet for the size fly you're casting. If the tippet gets shorter than two feet or so, cut it off and tie on a new one before trying to fool trout sipping insects on flat water.

A careful presentation is the most important element in fishing any smooth water.

Fishing the Dry Fly to the Banks

Most bank water is not worth fishing. It lacks depth for cover, and current to deliver food. Where you find a bank that drops off abruptly two to three feet deep, with a current that is not boiling but is brisk enough to escort food along, you'll find waiting trout. Many of the best holding banks are studded with fallen boulders, or have undercuts and indentations. Where overhanging brush protects such lies, they're more difficult to fish, but much more likely to hold large trout.

Your approach to such bank water should be from downstream. Rock-hop along the shore, staying out of the water if you can. If you've got to get in, then stay as close to shore as you can, and avoid sending any wading waves ahead of you. Fish upstream, with short casts: 20 to 30 feet. With longer casts, you cannot place the fly precisely enough.

Each cast should be made tight to the bank: from a few inches to no more than three feet out. Farther out than that and you're fishing lies, not bank water. Of course, if good lies such as boulders show up out there, you'd be foolish to pass them up. Fish both above and below them.

Often the current along the bank reverses itself in an eddy, flowing upstream rather than downstream right along the rocks and grasses. In this case, you also want to reverse your approach: face downstream in order to make your cast upstream into the reverse current.

Searching dry flies work well along the banks. Trout see lots of variety tumble in from shore. They also make quick decisions. They'll take high-floating and visible dressings. In salmonfly time, you'll do best with an Improved Sofa Pillow or Stimulator. In caddis time, choose an Elk Hair Caddis or Deer Hair Caddis. When hoppers are out, fish bank water with grasshopper patterns.

Fishing Banks From A Boat With A Dry Fly: Friction slows the current tight against the bank, where you want your dry to drift. The water out where you drift in your boat moves faster. Because of this, cast a dry fly ahead of the boat, so that the boat slowly catches up with it. This gives you slack and a long drag-free drift. If you cast behind the boat, its relative speed will draw your line tight, and you'll have drag almost instantly.

Keep one eye out for potential holding lies coming up. Keep the other eye on your drifting fly. Fishing a dry from a boat gives you somewhat of a split personality. It's a great way to make contact with some of the largest trout in any river.

Dry Fly Fishing Small Streams

Small streams are microcosms of larger trout streams and rivers. They are perfect places to learn how to read water and find fish. You'll quickly discover the kinds of water trout prefer,

and the kinds they don't. If you have such a stream nearby, fish it often. What you learn there will help you wherever else in the world you travel to fish.

Most dry fly casts to small streams are over plunge pools and pockets, to short but brisk glides and runs, and to tiny pockets along undercut banks.

It is tempting, when fishing plunge pools, to make your first casts up by the current tongue where the water dives in. That can be a mistake. Trout in small streams drift back down toward the tails of these pools, especially in summer when terrestrials fall to the water. If you step in and wade to the head of the pool, you'll spook them. Instead, approach from below the pool, at a stoop, and set your first cast onto the tail end of the pool. Work subsequent casts over all the water until you reach the current tongue. Dance your dry down that. It's the most productive spot. With any luck, you can take two or three trout before you reach the head of the pool.

Fish pocket water, glides, and runs the same way. Start at the lower end, and work upstream. Don't make more than two or three casts on any part of a tiny pool or pocket unless you've already had a hit. Trout make quick decisions in small streams. A few casts will bring them up if they're there and if they're willing. If not, keep moving, moving.

For most small stream fishing, searching dries are perfect. Keep them around size 12 to 14, not much larger. If some natural is around and predominant, imitate it as nearly as you can.

Dry Fly Pattern Styles

Beetle Bug

Yellow Parachute

Elk Hair Caddis

Bucktail Caddis

The Dry Fly on Large Rivers

The key to fishing large rivers with dry flies is to look for water that holds trout, and at the same time is shallow enough that they'll be willing to rise to the surface. That eliminates most deep pools. Instead, look for riffles and shallow runs, and fish them exactly as you would on smaller streams. Pattern the water to cover all hidden holding lies. Fish carefully to any obvious prime lies, like boulders.

Be especially careful to watch for rising fish on big rivers. No matter how deep the water they're working, if trout are rising, they're obviously susceptible to dry flies.

The edges of big rivers are obvious prime lies when you want to fish dries. Not all edge water holds fish (see page 36). But all fish holding along the edges are there because of the productivity of the shoreline vegetation. Most of what they eat lands on the surface from shore, so they're always looking up, and are primed for dries.

Gear for Big Water: It seems at first glance that you would always want your big gear—your searching rod—for fishing a big river. It's often true, but it's not always true. A lot of the time, you'll be fishing bushy searching dries on broad riffles, or tight to the banks, and you'll need your searching rod. Just as often, you'll be scouting out flats and tailouts where trout feed on tiny insects. When this is true, you'll want your light outfit for delicate presentations.

Always choose your gear based on the type of fishing you expect to be doing, not on the size water where you expect to be doing it.

Fishing Spring Creeks with Dry Flies

Spring creeks, because of their gentle and steady flows, usually allow trailing weedbeds to take root. These weeds harbor prolific aquatic insect populations, which hatch and cause trout to feed selectively. By their nature, spring creeks offer finesse fishing, usually over rising trout.

to match that food form. Second, you must move into the right position for the perfect presentation. On spring creeks, as on any other dry fly water, pay careful attention to the two halves of matching a hatch: imitation and presentation. If you try to separate them, you're bound to fail.

Your imitation rarely needs to be exact. Come as close as you can to the natural in size, then in form, and finally in color. If you don't have a matching pattern in your fly boxes, try trimming a fly that you already carry.

Your presentation needs to be as precise and delicate as possible. Obviously, for this kind of fishing, you'll want to be using your light outfit: a long rod that carries a three or four weight line. Your leader should be long; the tippet should be fine. Your cast should never line the fish. Most of the time, rely on the cross-stream reach cast or the downstream wiggle cast.

Mastery of the downstream wiggle cast will improve your success on spring creeks more than any other single factor.

Your approach to a spring creek is fairly well defined for you: watch the water, looking for rises. Once you've located a working trout, you must first observe what it is eating, then try

You will discover, in situation after situation, that you get refusals to upstream casts over any smooth water. If you turn around, and fish downstream so that trout see your fly well ahead of the line and leader, those same trout will often accept the same fly that they refused consistently, just moments earlier.

Sampling Kit: A small sampling kit takes up little room in your vest, yet can be vital to your spring creek fishing. Carry a small aquarium net, a jar lid with white inside, a pair of tweezers, a magnifying glass, and a few vials filled with 70 percent ethanol. That's all. You can swizzle a stomach sample in the jar lid to see what a selective trout has been eating, or lift a drifting insect right out of the surface film with the aquarium net.

You'll be surprised how often close observation tells you that you've been way off base in your dry fly selection. It can get you back on track instantly.

Seasonal and Daily Rhythms

When dry fly fishing, it's important to pay attention to the rhythms of the stream. Given a choice, you want to be fishing when trout are most willing to strike up to the surface.

In winter, insects will hatch and trout will sip at them only during the warmest parts of the warmest days. If you've got cabin fever, and the sun comes out, go fishing whenever the air warms up to 45 degrees or so, even if snow lies along the banks. Midges and some early stoneflies get active. It's no sure thing, but trout might get active, too.

In early spring, insects and trout are still most active during the warmest part of the day. Expect hatches and rising fish beginning just after noon. Activity usually ends around 3:00 p.m., when the sun tips over and things begin to cool. As spring warms up, the period of activity extends in both directions, starting as early as 9:00 a.m. and ending as late as 5:00 or 6:00 o'clock.

In summer, the period of most intense activity begins to shift from mid-day to the cooler parts of the day: morning and evening. If the summer is very hot, it might be wise to be on the stream at dawn. Activity lasts as late as 10:00 a.m.. Things shut down in the heat of the day until 5:00 or 6:00 p.m., and last from then until dark. Of course, if the day is cloudy and cool, or if the elevation is high and the stream temperature around 60 degrees or lower, trout will continue to be active through the middle of the day.

In fall, as temperatures drop, trout swing back to their spring schedule. They are most active at mid-day, least active at dawn and dusk.

Trout activity usually hinges on the activity of trout food. You can gauge the best times to fish by watching the insects: when they're getting into the most trouble on and around the water, that's when trout will be most active and most willing to feed.

Getting a feel for the rythm of the season and the day becomes extremely important on lakes.

Weather and the Dry Fly

It has already been pointed out that the best conditions for dry fly fishing prompt a sort of liveliness in and around the water. In winter, spring, and fall, things are most lively when the air temperature is fairly high, when the sun is out and igniting things.

In the warmth of late spring, summer, and early fall, a cool day can enliven things much more than another hot, sunny day. A cooling shot of rain can perk a river up for several days, until weather patterns return to normal. It would be common, at these times of year, to have good dry fly fishing right in the rain so long as the rain does not cause the river to rise.

Many aquatic insect types prefer to hatch on cloudy, overcast days. Most mayfly species, for example, come off in greater numbers, and for longer periods, during a drizzle. Experienced dry fly fishermen glance at a gloomy, low sky and get cheerful. Even if the day brings some rain, they know that the hatches will be on for several hours rather than just one or two. Trout key on the insects, so they'll remain active on an overcast day far longer than they will on a bright day, especially in mid- summer.

Chapter 6

Fishing Dry Flies on Lakes and Ponds

When trout are more than six to eight feet deep in lakes, they are not likely to rise all the way to the top for a dry fly, no matter how enticing it might be. So your first step toward catching trout from lakes on dry flies is to find them in shallow water. Lakes and ponds have the same seasonal cycle. An awareness of it will tell you when trout are likely to be shallow, and when they'll be deep.

Cycle of the Seasons: In winter, the water is cold. Insects and other food forms are inactive. Trout are down deep and have little interest in dry flies. The exception might be during a winter midge hatch on a warm day. If you see rises, you might take them on dries. It's rare.

In spring and early summer, insects reach peak activity. Trout follow their emergences into the shallows, and feed on them heavily. It's the time when the dry fly fisherman should also reach his peak activity on lakes and ponds.

In middle to late summer and early fall, the water is warm and becomes stratified. The coolest water is down 15 to 25 feet. Trout go down there, too, and are not often near enough to the surface to take dries, except sometimes at dawn after a cool night.

At fall turnover, cool water rushes to the top. All sorts of food forms follow it, and trout do, too. For a few weeks, dry fly fishing can be nearly as good as in spring. Then the water begins to cool again, and trout drop down toward winter depths.

Finding Trout Susceptible to Dry Flies: When the time of year is right, next you've got to locate specific stillwater areas where trout are most likely to take dries. The most obvious way to find them, in water of any depth, is to spot the rise rings of feeding trout. Any time you see rising trout, it's prime time to fish with a dry fly. Because trout will often be somewhat selective when they're rising, you'll want to collect a natural and try to match it as closely as you can.

When trout are not rising, they're usually down near the bottom. Restrict your dry fly fishing to the shoreline, and to all of the edge water out to about six feet deep. Beyond that, you're wasting your time, most of the time, fishing a dry fly.

Shoals and weedbeds, far out from the shoreline, can be productive places if they are shallow enough, again around three to six feet deep. Trout will cruise along the bottom or just above the tops of weeds. If an insect, or a dry fly, lands on top, they'll spear up to take it. Weedbeds and shoals are often difficult to spot. Wear polaroid sunglasses, and scan the surface looking for areas that are darker than the rest of the water. The dark surface usually means a shallow bottom or a weed patch down below.

Confine stillwater dry fly fishing to edges and shallows.

Fly Pattern Selection for Lakes and Ponds

Carry your stream fly boxes, but develop a small list of dry flies that give you confidence when you fish them on lakes and ponds. Start with the dressings that have worked for you on streams and rivers, for example the Adams, Elk Hair Caddis and Humpy. Experiment with others. Whenever you have success on a fly, make a mental note of it. Try that fly again when conditions become similar, but also when they're different. The idea is to work up a few flies that you can rely on. Confidence in a fly is half of what makes it take trout, because you'll fish it with expectation and concentration.

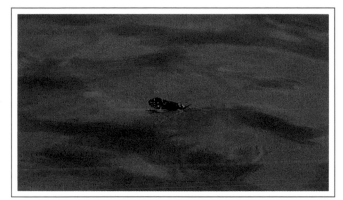

Traveling sedge . . .

After you've developed a list of basics, similar to the searching flies used on streams, then it's time to begin looking at what trout eat in stillwaters, and develop a second list of hatch-matching dry flies. This will take time. There's no hurry. When you hit a hatch, try to find a fly that

. . . and its imitation, the Mikulak sedge.

takes trout. Then the next time you arrive at a lake or pond and find the same hatch happening, you'll have a fly that assures you some success.

Over the years you'll find that you've added some midge patterns such as the Griffith's Gnat, a few mayfly dressings like the Olive Harrop Hairwing Dun and the Olive Comparadun, specific caddis dressings like the Mikulak Sedge. Observe the naturals, then look at the fly plates on pages 51 through 56. Choose the nearest fly you can find to the natural. If you tie flies, you might create your own. Ask local guides and fly shop clerks what works best on specific waters.

Your list of dressings should be tuned to the waters you fish. At first it will be similar to the list everybody else uses. But it should end up all your own, and it should help you take lake and pond trout on dry flies when other anglers around you fail.

Dry Fly Tactics for Lakes and Ponds: Tactics for fishing still waters with dry flies are few, and simple. If fish are rising, cast to the rise rings and let the fly sit. Don't make the mistake of picking the fly up and constantly pasting it into every new rise. That will put the trout down. Let it sit awhile; give the fish time to find it.

If a single fish is moving and rising, try to calculate the direction of its next rise. Place the fly ahead of it, and wait for it to arrive. If you see just a single rise, place the first cast on it, the second cast 10 feet or so to one side, the third cast the same distance in the opposite direction, trying to intercept its travels.

If no trout are rising, the dry fly is most effective when fished to the shoreline, to any visible cover, or above shoals and weedbeds. Cast within a foot or two of shore. Let the fly sit. Cast next to any floating or submerged logs, limbs, or brush. Place the fly next to lily pads, and at the edges of reed patches.

Always make your first strategy the still dry fly. Let it rest; let trout find it. Don't ever stick with the same thing forever if it fails to take trout. Instead, twitch the fly, or even skitter it over the surface. Certain caddis species, called traveling sedges, motor around on the water. If they're around, or even if trout can remember when they have been, the skittered fly will cause more detonations than one left to sit.

Vary your strategy according to the situation. If trout are cruising and sipping in shallows, keep out of sight, don't make wading waves, place your fly delicately ahead of them. If they're milling and rising in a pod, cast the fly to the edge of the pod and let the trout find it. If they're holding around cover, and not moving, then place your fly in or near the cover, let it sit a moment, then skate it a little to entice the trout.

Try different methods. You'll soon find the one that works best.

Chapter 7

※

Hatches and Patterns

When trout feed selectively, on either lake or stream, it can be frustrating. Often they'll refuse everything you throw at them. Even the most experienced fly fishing writers, though they neglect to admit it in print, sometimes fail to solve such situations. The key to catching rising trout is observation. At times you'll have to make several observations, and run through a minor litany of changes, before you come up with the combination that fools the fish.

The basic steps in successfully matching a hatch.

Step 1: Reading Rise Forms. Observe the rise form of a feeding fish. If a bubble is left in the rings of the rise, the trout has taken something off the surface, and it's time to fish a dry fly. If you see no bubble, suspect that the fish has taken something beneath the surface. You'll need to switch from dries to emergers (see page 50), or else to wet flies or nymphs.

Step 2: Observing Insects. Observe the insect the trout are eating, as closely as you can. You might be able to do this with a close look at the water—get your nose right down to it. A pair of small binoculars will often let you spy into the feeding lane of a rising trout without disturbing it. Sometimes you've got to wade out and spook the fish, then suspend a collecting net in the current to get a look at what the trout has been eating. Wade back out and wait for the trout to begin rising again.

If more than one insect species is hatching, be sure to notice which the trout prefer. When you've discovered which insect interests them, make sure you notice whether they take the emerger, dun, or spinner.

Step 3: Selecting A Fly Pattern. Once you hold the insect in your hand, choose a fly from your boxes that is closest to it in size, form and color in that order. If anything, go one size smaller, but never one size larger. Be sure the form is right when the fly sits on the water. If it looks right to you from casting distance, it will look right to the trout a surprising percentage of the time, no matter what it looks like when held in your hand. Get the color as close as you can, but it is the least of the three factors. Trout will often accept a fly far off in color so long as the size and shape are right.

Step 4: Refine Your Gear. Be sure your tackle, and especially your tippet, suit the fly size, and the fishing situation. Use your light presentation outfit when matching hatches. If your tippet is too short or too heavy, lengthen it and fine it down.

Step 5: Choose the Correct Casting Position and Presentation: Get as many conflicting currents behind you as possible. Then choose the best presentation. Most of the time, you'll use either the up-and-across presentation, the cross-stream reach cast, or the downstream wiggle cast. At times you'll be creative and use a combination of a couple of these, followed by a series of mends.

Mayflies and Pattern Styles

Mayfly duns have historically been the prime insect of interest to dry fly fishermen. Mayflies live in all water types that hold trout. The duns emerge in heavy hatches out in open

water, where trout can get at them. Trout feed on mayfly duns greedily, and often selectively.

Mayflies are delicate and beautiful. With their upright wings and slender, tipped-up bodies, they resemble sprit-rigged sailboats. They range in size from a giant size 4 down to a tiny size 26. Most are size 12 to 16. Their colors range from drab green to bright yellow. The most common colors are olive, gray, and sulphur.

Before choosing a dressing style to match mayfly duns, consider the water where you'll fish it. Some species live and hatch in fast water. You'll need hackled patterns to match

them, or the flies won't float. Other species live in smooth water. Patterns without hackles float well enough, and have silhouettes more like the naturals. Wherever the water is rough, choose a fly style for flotation. Where the water is smooth, choose a fly style for exact imitation.

Once you've chosen a mayfly pattern style, then it's a simple matter to observe the specimen the trout are eating at the moment, and to pick out a specific dressing that is closest to it in size and color. The best approach to matching mayflies is to pick a couple of pattern styles, one for fast water and one for slow, then tie or buy a few size and color variations to cover the hatches you encounter.

A good start would be the Adams, Blue-winged Olive, and Light Cahill, all hackled, all in size 12 through 16. Add either Comparaduns or Harrop Hairwing Duns in olive, sulphur, and gray, sizes 14 through 18, for smooth water. That small box of flies would match most mayfly hatches, on most waters.

Matching Mayfly Spinners: The reproductive stage of the mayfly is called the spinner. They are not the same color as the duns from which they molt. Female spinners lay their eggs on the water, and fall to it spent. Their wings are usually spread on the surface, and your fly style must imitate this. Again, you've got to observe them in order to match them. You can tie or buy spinner imitations with wings of Polypropylene yarn, hen hackle tips, or rooster hackle wound in normal fashion and clipped on the top and bottom. Hackle stems make excellent bodies for these slender insects.

The most common sizes are 12 to 16. The most common colors are olive, tan, gray, and rusty red.

Mayfly Pattern Styles

Sparkle Dun

Harrop Dun

Catskill Dry

No-hackle Dry

Caddisflies and Pattern Styles

Caddis hatch sporadically, and more often at nightfall. They are less visible than mayflies, and are less often noticed by dry fly fishermen. In their various stages, it's likely they are eaten more often by trout. They have adapted to an even wider variety of waters, and are not so reliant on perfect water quality. As a consequence, they are becoming more important than mayflies as time goes on, and as average water quality degrades.

Adult caddis have tent-shaped wings, held over bulbous bodies that are not quite as long as the wings. All of the species in the order have the same shape, though they vary from giant size 4 down to microcaddis too small to imitate. Colors range from bright tannish-yellow to black. The most common sizes are 12 to 16, the most common colors gray and tannish-brown.

It's wise to pick a couple of pattern styles for the caddis, one with excellent flotation for fast water, another displaying an accurate wing silhouette for slow water. The Elk Hair Caddis is the standard fly for caddis hatches. It is excellent all across the country. It sits perkily on its hackle tips, and rides out the roughest water. Leave the hackle off, or clip it when you come to smooth water, and it shows off the body and wing silhouettes, thus serving well on all water types. It is probably the most popular searching dressing in all of dry fly fishing.

The Elk Hair Caddis and its spinoff, the Deer Hair Caddis, cover most trout stream caddis hatches. Carry these in sizes 12 through 16.

The Quill-wing Caddis has a more natural wing silhouette, and should be carried for smooth-water situations. Versions with tan bodies and brown wings, plus olive bodies with gray wings, cover most hatches. Carry them in sizes 12 through 16.

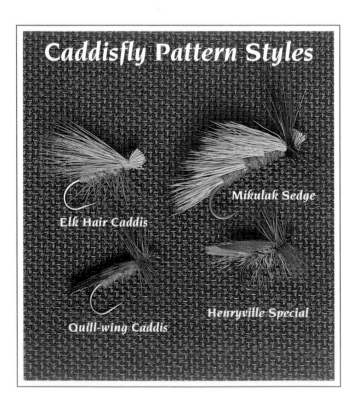

Caddis Behavior: Adult caddis often scoot across the water, especially on lakes and ponds. While the drag-free drift is usually best, it can fail to interest trout. When it does, the fish might be accustomed to seeing the naturals skating on the surface. If the standard presentation doesn't work, try giving your caddis dry a little movement on the surface: hop it an inch or two. At times, you'll want to get upstream, cast downstream, and dangle the fly on a short line. Skate it on the surface, alternating the movement with a foot or two of free drift.

Stoneflies and Pattern Styles

Mayflies, caddisflies, and stoneflies are the big three of the aquatic insect orders. In terms of importance to trout fishermen, stoneflies are the least of the big three. They do not emerge out in open water, like mayflies and most caddis, where trout can get at them readily. Instead, most stonefly species migrate

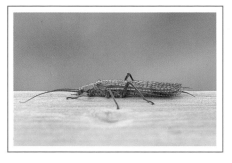

across the bottom as nymphs, and crawl out on shore to emerge as adults where trout can't get at them.

Stonefly adults do hang out on grasses and vegetation along the edges of streams, where they often fall to the water. They're also available in midstream when they return to the water to lay their eggs. Many are very large meals for trout. When they are available, trout key on them. You need to carry a few imitations to enjoy much success when trout feed on them.

Unlike mayflies and caddis, which tend toward average sizes and colors, the important stonefly groups are widely divergent, though they share the same shape. They run from little brown stones, at size 16, up to giant salmon flies, two inches long and imitated with flies tied on size 4 hooks. Other important groups include the golden stones, about size 6 or 8, and the little yellow stones, size 10 and 12.

The best pattern style for the stonefly group incorporates a good silhouette of the natural with lots of hackle for flotation. The Improved Sofa Pillow, tied in sizes 4 and 6, works well for the giant salmon fly hatch. The similar Stimulator imitates golden stones in sizes 6 and 8. Variations on the same theme, tied or purchased in the right sizes and colors, work as well for the smaller yellow and brown stones, and even for the little green stone wherever it is found to be important.

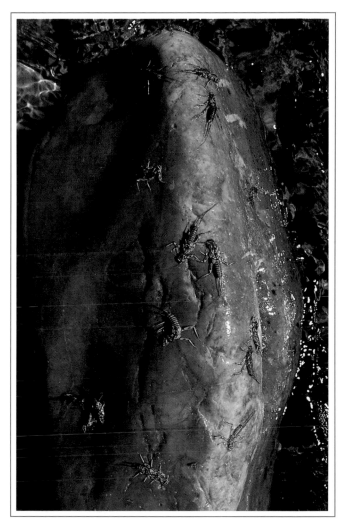

Stonefly Pattern Styles

Stimulator

Improved Sofa Pillow

Sofa Pillow

Clark's Stone Fly

Stonefly Strategy: The nymphs of most stonefly species are found in the fastest riffles and runs: water that contains lots of oxygen. The adults hang around near such water, and return to it to deposit their eggs. In order to fish their imitations over rough water, you'll usually want to arm yourself with your searching outfit. Build your leaders to suit the size and wind resistance of the flies.

Since most of your stonefly fishing will be over fairly fast water, upstream presentations are the usual rule. Fish tight to bank water, especially where you see salmon flies and golden stones clamboring about in streamside grasses and willows. Trout wait wherever the water is deep enough to conceal them. When a natural stonefly, or your imitation, lands on the water above them, they detonate on it.

Midges and Pattern Styles

The word midge takes on two meanings. In the oldest use, a midge is any tiny fly, say size 16 and smaller. In the newest and most common use among those who study insects and match hatches with dry flies, the term refers to members of the Chironomidae family of insects: the midges. The latter meaning is more precise, and the one used here.

Not all midges are small. Some chironomids are as large as size 10. Most midge species fall in the range between size 16 and 22. They live in lakes and ponds, and in the slowest reaches of running water. You will usually fish their tiny imitations on smooth water, over selectively rising trout.

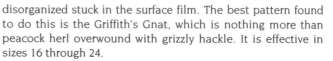

The surface film of slow or still water can be quite a barrier to a tiny insect. Midges often get stuck when trying to emerge; they can't quite wriggle through the film to escape their shucks. As a consequence, patterns for what is termed the stillborn stage become very important. They imitate something small and disorganized stuck in the surface film. The best pattern found to do this is the Griffith's Gnat, which is nothing more than peacock herl overwound with grizzly hackle. It is effective in sizes 16 through 24.

Fully emerged midges are important at times, and you should carry at least a few imitations of them. Because they are so small, and have such whisps for wings, their imitations can be simple: just a tail, thread body, and sparse hackle. Tie or buy them in gray, tan, and green, sizes 18 through 22, and you'll have most midge situations solved.

Observation is always the key when trout feed on such tiny creatures. Use your collecting net to strain the surface currents. Examine its meshes closely to see exactly what the trout might be taking.

Often, when midges hatch, trout take them in clusters. It's a lot easier, from your point of view, to imitate half a dozen midges stuck together than it is to imitate them one at a time. For that reason, it helps to carry a few standard dry fly dressings tied with hackles wound over the bodies, to make them look like a conglomerated mass of midges. The most successful is the Palmered Adams, in size 14 to 18.

Midge Pattern Styles

Palmered Adams Midge   Mosquito Midge

Tan Midge   Griffith's Gnat

Terrestrials and Matching Patterns

A trout makes most of its living eating aquatic insects. You won't fish far into summer before bumping into trout nipping at insects that fall to the water from streamside grasses and vegetation. These land-borne insects are called terrestials.

When trout see a wide variety of terrestrial insects arriving on the water, they do not become selective to any particular one of them. At such times, you can usually take fish on your favorite searching dries. When a single species of terrestrial becomes dominant, however, and trout see little else, they tend to get selective. That's when it helps to capture a specimen and note its size, form, and color before selecting a pattern to match it.

If the water is smooth you might have to get your nose right down to the water to notice what the trout are taking. Better yet, get out your aquarium net and let it sift the surface currents for a few minutes. Then lift it out and take a close look. Sometimes it will seethe with tiny beetles or ants.

The most common terrestrials are grasshoppers. They get onto the water wherever grasses grow along the stream. Because they are such a large mouthful, trout get greedy for them, and will gallop to get them even when only a few are around. If you see hoppers in the grass, especially on warm, windy days, try a Letort Hopper or Dave Whitlock's Hopper in size 8 through 14. Use a dead drift float. Don't hesitate to

smack your fly to the water if that's what it takes to attract the attention of the trout.

Beetles and ants tend to be much smaller. Trout usually sip them rather than rushing them. You'll have to use small flies, and fish them with delicate presentations. On the kinds of smooth water where ants and beetles are important, you'll want to refine your tackle and tippets, and employ the reach cast and downstream wiggle cast for most of your fishing. Choose patterns that resemble the naturals in size and shape, and also roughly in color. Most of the time they will be Black Beetles in size 14 through 18, or Black and Cinnamon Ants in sizes 16 through 20.

Fishing Emergers

Some insect types, mostly tiny mayflies and midges, brace themselves against the surface film and get stuck there, unable to escape their nymphal or pupal shucks and fly away as adults. Trout know about this problem. When lots of a single small species hatches, trout sometimes key on the cripples, and ignore imitations of the adults. When this happens you've got to fish a floating emerger pattern to take trout.

This behavior happens only in a narrow range of circumstances. The surface film is a barrier only on smooth water: spring creek flats, and also lakes and ponds. The film is a barrier only to the tiniest of insects. Anything size 14 and up has enough mass to break through it quickly. You'll only fish emerger patterns on smooth water, during hatches of tiny insects: mayflies and midges.

Your imitations should look roughly like the nymphs or the pupae from which the adults arise, with half-formed wings added. Or they should look roughly like the adults themselves, with something added to imitate the trailing shucks. The Olive Sparkle Dun and Pale Morning Sparkle Duns are examples. Use your aquarium net to collect and examine stillborn naturals. Use your imagination to select flies that match them.

The world of trout and insects holds too many surprises to cover all of the possibilities in any one book. For example, minor orders such as alderflies sometimes cause selective feeding on streams, and others such as damselflies can cause selective feeding on lakes and ponds.

It is not important to memorize all of these in advance. It is important to be aware that there are other insects out there, that trout feed on them selectively at times, and that you might encounter a situation where you've got to match them to enjoy much success. It's easy enough to solve such situations so long as you remember to observe what's going on around you, and recall that the pattern you select should be the nearest you can find to the natural in terms of size, form, and color.

Emergers should be imitated with dressings that feature the trailing shuck, such as the Olive or Pale Morning Sparkle Dun.

Minor insect orders, such as this damselfly adult, often entice rising trout, and catch you by surprise on stream, lake, or pond.

Chapter 8

Dry Fly Dressings

Adams

Hook: Standard dry fly, sizes 10-18
Thread: Black 6/0
Wings: Grizzly hen hackle tips
Tail: Brown and grizzly hackle fibers, mixed
Body: Gray muskrat underfur
Hackle: Brown and grizzly hackle, mixed

Parachute Adams

Hook: Standard dry fly, sizes 12-18
Thread: Black 6/0
Wingpost: White calf body hair
Tail: Grizzly hackle fibers
Body: Gray muskrat underfur
Hackle: Brown and grizzly hackle, parachute

Yellow Parachute

Hook: Standard dry fly, sizes 10-16
Thread: Brown 6/0
Wingpost: Yellow Polypro yarn
Tail: Brown hackle fibers
Body: Hare's mask fur or synthetic
Hackle: Brown, parachute

Elk Hair Caddis

Hook: Standard dry fly, sizes 10-18
Thread: Tan 6/0
Rib: Gold wire counterwound over body and hackle
Body: Hare's ear fur or synthetic
Hackle: Ginger, palmered over body
Wing: Tan elk hair

Deer Hair Caddis

Hook: Standard dry fly, sizes 10-18
Thread: Olive 6/0
Body: Olive fur or synthetic
Hackle: Blue dun
Wing: Natural dun deer hair

Attractor Dry Flies

Bucktail Caddis

Hook: Standard dry fly, sizes 10-16
Thread: Black 6/0
Tail: Deer body hair
Hackle: Brown, palmered over body
Body: Yellow yarn
Wing: Deer hair

Blue-winged Olive

Hook: Standard dry fly, sizes 12-20
Thread: Olive 6/0
Wing: Blue dun hackle tips
Tail: Blue dun hackle fibers
Body: Brownish-olive fur or synthetic
Hackle: Blue dun

Blue Dun

Hook: Standard dry fly, sizes 12-18
Thread: Gray 6/0
Wing: Mallard quill, upright and divided
Tail: Blue dun hackle fibers
Body: Muskrat fur
Hackle: Blue dun

Dark Hendrickson

Hook: Standard dry fly, sizes 12-18
Thread: Gray 6/0
Wings: Lemon woodduck flank fibers
Tail: Dark blue dun hackle fibers
Body: Dark gray muskrat fur
Hackle: Dark blue dun

Light Hendrickson

Hook: Standard dry fly, sizes 12-18
Thread: Tan 6/0
Wings: Lemon woodduck flank fibers
Tail: Medium blue dun hackle fibers
Body: Pinkish fox belly fur or synthetic
Hackle: Medium blue dun

Dark Cahill

Hook: Standard dry fly, sizes 12-18
Thread: Tan 6/0
Wings: Lemon woodduck flank fibers
Tail: Dark ginger hackle fibers
Body: Gray muskrat fur
Hackle: Dark ginger

Light Cahill

Hook: Standard dry fly, sizes 12-18
Thread: Cream 6/0
Wings: Lemon woodduck flank fibers
Tail: Light ginger hackle fibers
Body: Cream badger underfur or synthetic
Hackle: Light ginger

Ginger Quill

Hook: Standard dry fly, sizes 12-18
Thread: Yellow 6/0
Wings: Natural gray duck quill
Tail: Golden ginger hackle fibers
Body: Stripped peacock quill
Hackle: Golden ginger

Quill Gordon

Hook: Standard dry fly, sizes 12-14
Thread: Black 6/0
Wings: Lemon woodduck flank fibers
Tail: Dark blue dun hackle fibers
Body: Stripped peacock quill
Hackle: Dark blue dun

Royal Coachman

Hook: Standard dry fly, sizes 10-16
Thread: Black 6/0
Wing: White duck quill
Tail: Golden pheasant tippet fibers
Butt: Peacock herl
Body: Red floss
Shoulder: Peacock herl
Hackle: Coachman brown

Renegade

Hook: Standard dry fly, sizes 8-16
Thread: Black 6/0
Tip: Fine flat gold tinsel
Rear hackle: Brown
Body: Peacock herl
Front hackle: White

Royal Wulff

Hook: Standard dry fly, sizes 6-16
Thread: Black 6/0
Wings: White calftail or calf body hair
Tail: Moose body hair
Butt: Peacock herl
Body: Red floss
Shoulder: Peacock herl
Hackle: Coachman brown

Grizzly Wulff

Hook: Standard dry fly, sizes 8-14
Thread: Black 6/0
Wings: Natural brown bucktail
Tail: Natural brown bucktail
Body: Yellow floss
Hackle: Brown and grizzly, mixed

Humpy

Hook: Standard dry fly, sizes 6-16
Thread: Yellow 6/0
Tail: Deer body hair
Underbody: Yellow thread over butts of body and wing hair
Overbody: Wing deer hair pulled forward
Wing: Deer hair, upright and divided
Hackle: Grizzly and brown, mixed

Royal Trude

Hook: Standard dry fly, sizes 6-16
Thread: Black 6/0
Tail: Golden pheasant tippet fibers
Butt: Peacock herl
Body: Red floss
Shoulder: Peacock herl
Wing: White calf tail
Hackle: Coachman brown

House and Lot Variant

Hook: Standard dry fly, sizes 10-14
Thread: Black 6/0
Wings: White calf tail, upright and divided
Tail: White calf body hair
Rib: Fine gold wire, reverse wrapped
Body: Rear half stripped peacock quill; front half peacock herl.
Hackle: Badger

Sofa Pillow

Hook: 3X long, sizes 4-10
Thread: Brown 6/0
Tail: Red goose quill
Body: Red floss
Wing: Red fox squirrel tail
Hackle: Brown saddle.

Improved Sofa Pillow

Hook: 3X long, sizes 4-10
Thread: Black 6/0
Tail: Natural elk hair
Rib: Brown hackle, undersized
Body: Orange wool yarn
Wing: Natural elk hair
Hackle: Brown saddle

Clark's Stonefly

Hook: 3X long, sizes 6-10
Thread: Orange 6/0
Body: Flat gold tinsel
Underwing: Rust and gold macrame yarn, combed and mixed
Wing: Moose body hair
Hackle: Brown saddle

Stimulator

Hook: 3X long, sizes 6-10
Thread: Fluorescent orange 6/0
Tail: Deer body hair
Rib: Grizzly hackle
Body: Yellow fur or synthetic
Wing: Deer body hair
Hackle: Grizzly, palmered over thorax
Thorax: Orange fur or synthetic

Little Brown Stone

Hook: 3X long, sizes 12-16
Thread: Brown 6/0
Tail: Ringneck pheasant body fibers
Rib: Brown thread
Body: Seal brown synthetic yarn
Wing: Single grizzly hackle tip
Hackle: Grizzly

Little Yellow Stone

Hook: 3X long, sizes 12-14
Thread: Yellow 6/0
Rib: Ginger hackle
Body: Gold yarn or fur
Wing: Golden bucktail
Hackle: Ginger

Little Green Stone

Hook: 3X long, sizes 14-16
Thread: Olive 6/0
Rib: Olive hackle
Body: Green floss or fur
Wing: Green bucktail
Hackle: Green

Letort Hopper

Hook: 2X long, sizes 8-14
Thread: Yellow 6/0
Body: Yellow fur or synthetic
Underwing: Mottled turkey quill
Overwing: Natural deer hair
Head: Natural deer hair, spun and clipped

Dave Whitlock's Hopper

Hook: 2X long, sizes 4-12
Thread: Gray 6/0
Tail: Red deer hair; small loop yellow yarn
Body: Yellow wool yarn
Hackle: Brown, clipped and palmered
Underwing: Yellow calf tail
Overwing: Turkey wing quill, lacquered
Legs: Dyed yellow grizzly hackle stems, knotted
Collar: Tan deer hair, spun
Head: Tan deer hair, spun and clipped

Blue-wing Olive No-hackle

Hook: Extra fine dry fly, sizes 14-20
Thread: Olive 6/0
Tails: Blue dun hackle fibers, split
Body: Olive fur or synthetic
Wings: Teal quill sections

Olive Harrop Hairwing Dun

Hook: Standard dry fly, sizes 12-20
Thread: Olive 6/0
Tail: Blue dun hackle fibers, split
Body: Olive fur or synthetic
Hackle: Blue dun, clipped on bottom
Wing: Gray deer hair

Sulphur Harrop Hairwing Dun

Hook: Standard dry fly, sizes 12-18
Thread: Pale yellow
Tail: Light ginger hackle fibers, split
Body: Pale yellow fur or synthetic
Hackle: Ginger, clipped on bottom
Wing: Bleached deer hair

Gray Harrop Hairwing Dun

Hook: Standard dry fly, sizes 12-16
Thread: Gray 6/0
Tail: Blue dun hackle fibers, split
Body: Muskrat fur
Hackle: Blue dun, clipped on bottom
Wing: Gray deer hair

Blue Quill Spinner

Hook: Extra fine dry fly, sizes 12-16
Thread: Gray 6/0
Tail: Blue dun hackle fibers, split
Body: Blue dun hackle stem
Hackle: Blue dun and grizzly, mixed; clipped on bottom

Imitative Dry Flies

Red Quill Spinner

Hook: Extra fine dry fly, sizes 12-16
Thread: Red 6/0
Tails: Brown hackle fibers, split
Body: Brown hackle stem
Hackle: Brown and grizzly, mixed; clipped on bottom

Poly-Wing Spinner

Hook: Extra fine dry fly, sizes 18-22
Thread: Olive 6/0
Tails: White hackle fibers, split
Abdomen: Olive fur or synthetic
Wings: Gray Polypro yarn, tied spent
Thorax: Brown fur or synthetic

Little Olive Comparadun

Hook: Extra fine dry fly, sizes 16-20
Thread: Olive 6/0
Wing: Natural dun deer hair, flared 160 degrees
Tail: Blue dun hackle fibers, split
Body: Olive fur or synthetic

Pale Morning Comparadun

Hook: Extra fine dry fly, sizes 14-18
Thread: Pale yellow 6/0
Wing: Pale cream deer hair, flared 160 degrees
Tail: Ginger hackle fibers, split
Body: Yellow-olive fur or synthetic

March Brown Comparadun

Hook: Standard dry fly, sizes 12-16
Thread: Tan 6/0
Wing: Natural brown deer hair, flared 160 degrees
Tail: Brown hackle fibers, split
Body: Hare's mask fur or synthetic

Little Olive Thorax

Hook: Standard dry fly, sizes 14-20
Thread: Olive 6/0
Wing: Blue dun hen hackle fiber clump
Tail: Blue dun hackle fibers, split
Body: Olive fur or synthetic
Hackle: Blue dun, clipped on bottom

Sulphur Thorax

Hook: Standard dry fly, sizes 12-18
Thread: Pale yellow 6/0
Wing: Ginger hen hackle fiber clump
Tail: Ginger hackle fibers, split
Body: Yellow-olive fur or synthetic
Hackle: Ginger, clipped on bottom

Hendrickson Thorax

Hook: Standard dry fly, sizes 12-16
Thread: Olive 6/0
Wing: Dark blue dun hen hackle fiber clump
Tail: Blue dun hackle fibers, split
Body: Grayish-tan fox fur or synthetic
Hackle: Blue dun, clipped on bottom

Olive Sparkle Dun

Hook: Extra fine dry fly, sizes 14-20
Thread: Olive 6/0
Wing: Natural dun deer hair
Tail: Olive Zelon
Body: Olive fur or synthetic

Pale Morning Sparkle Dun

Hook: Extra fine dry fly, sizes 12-18
Thread: Pale yellow 6/0
Wing: Natural cream deer hair
Tail: Gray Zelon
Body: Yellow-olive fur or synthetic

Kings River Caddis

Hook: Standard dry fly, sizes 10-6
Thread: Brown 6/0
Body: Raccoon fur or grayish-brown synthetic
Wings: Mottled brown turkey quill
Hackle: Brown

Gray Quill-wing Caddis

Hook: Standard dry fly, sizes 10-16
Thread: Gray
Body: Muskrat fur
Wings: Mallard or goose wing quill
Hackle: Blue dun

Henryville Special

Hook: Standard dry fly, sizes 14-20
Thread: Black 6/0
Rib: Grizzly hackle, undersized, palmered
Body: Olive fur or synthetic
Underwing: Lemon woodduck flank fibers
Overwing: Mallard wing quill
Hackle: Dark ginger

Mikulak Sedge

Hook: 2X long, sizes 8-12
Thread: Black 6/0
Tail: Elk hair
Body: Olive fur or synthetic
Mid-wing: Elk hair
Wing: Elk hair
Hackle: Brown
Head: Butts of wing hair

Adams Midge

Hook: Standard dry fly, sizes 14-20
Thread: Black 6/0
Tail: Grizzly hackle fibers
Body: Muskrat fur
Hackle: Grizzly

Olive Midge

Hook: Standard dry fly, sizes 14-20
Thread: Olive 6/0
Tail: Blue dun hackle fibers
Body: Olive fur or synthetic
Hackle: Blue dun

Tan Midge

Hook: Standard dry fly, sizes 14-20
Thread: Tan 6/0
Tail: Ginger hackle fibers
Body: Tan fur or synthetic
Hackle: Ginger

Palmered Adams Midge

Hook: Standard dry fly, sizes 14-18
Thread: Black 6/0
Wings: Grizzly hen hackle tips
Tail: Grizzly hackle fibers
Rib: Grizzly hackle, palmered
Body: Muskrat fur
Hackle: Grizzly

Palmered Tan Midge

Hook: Standard dry fly, sizes 14-18
Thread: Tan 6/0
Wings: Ginger hen hackle tips
Tail: Ginger hackle fibers
Rib: Ginger hackle, palmered
Body: Tan fur or synthetic
Hackle: Ginger

Griffith's Gnat

Hook: Extra fine dry fly, sizes 16-22
Thread: Black 6/0
Hackle: Grizzly, palmered over body
Body: Peacock herl

Mosquito

Hook: Standard dry fly, sizes 14-18
Thread: Black 6/0
Wings: Grizzly hen hackle tips
Tail: Grizzly hackle fibers
Body: Dark and light moose mane fibers, wound together
Hackle: Grizzly

Black Fur Ant

Hook: Standard dry fly, sizes 14-20
Thread: Black 6/0
Abdomen: Black fur or synthetic
Hackle: Black
Thorax: Black fur or synthetic

Cinnamon Fur Ant

Hook: Standard dry fly, sizes 12-20
Thread: Tan 6/0
Abdomen: Cinnamon fur or synthetic
Hackle: Brown
Thorax: Cinnamon fur or synthetic

Black Beetle

Hook: Standard dry fly, sizes 12-18
Thread: Black 6/0
Shellback: Black deer body hair
Hackle: Black, palmered, trimmed on bottom
Body: Black fur or synthetic

Jassid

Hook: Standard dry fly, sizes 16-22
Thread: Black 6/0
Body: Black hackle, palmered, clipped top and bottom
Wing: Jungle cock eye or substitute